Smart Warehouse

Revolutionizing Storage and Distribution with Technology

Table of Contents

Introduction to Smart Warehousing	**5**
Core Technologies in Smart Warehouses	**14**
1. Detailed overview of technologies powering smart warehouses: IoT, AI, machine learning, robotics, and big data.	14
2. How these technologies interact within a warehouse setting.	14
3. Examples of major companies leading the way in implementing these technologies.	14
Warehouse Management Systems (WMS) and Smart Warehouse Software	**23**
1. Role of WMS in smart warehousing.	23
2. How WMS integrates with smart technology (IoT, AI, etc.) to enhance efficiency.	23
3. Key features of a smart WMS and selection considerations for businesses.	23
Automation in Warehousing: Robots, Drones, and AGVs	**32**
1. Types of warehouse automation: robotic arms, automated guided vehicles (AGVs), drones, and autonomous forklifts.	32
2. Advantages of using robotics and automation in warehouses.	32
3. Case studies on companies successfully implementing robotics.	32
Internet of Things (IoT) in Warehouse Management	**40**
1. How IoT enables smart inventory tracking, real-time data, and condition monitoring.	40
2. Impact of IoT on asset tracking, environmental monitoring, and equipment maintenance.	40
3. Security concerns and data privacy in IoT-enabled warehouses.	40
Artificial Intelligence and Data Analytics for Smart Warehouses	**48**
1. Role of AI in demand forecasting, inventory optimization, and workflow automation.	48
2. How predictive analytics improve decision-making and operational efficiency.	48
3. Use of AI-powered cameras and sensors for quality control and anomaly detection.	48
Digital Twins in Warehouse Operations	**56**
1. Explanation of digital twins and their role in warehouse management.	56
2. How digital twins enable virtual simulations, testing, and planning.	56
3. Real-world examples of digital twin applications in warehousing.	56
4. Procter & Gamble (P&G)	**61**
1. Techniques for automating and optimizing inventory management.	63
2. How smart warehouses achieve near-perfect inventory accuracy.	63
3. AI-driven demand forecasting for just-in-time inventory. please write minimum 2000 words about it	63
Energy-Efficient and Sustainable Smart Warehousing	**72**

1. Eco-friendly smart warehouse technologies: energy-efficient lighting, climate control, and renewable energy. 72
2. Benefits of sustainability in warehouses (cost-saving, eco-friendliness). 72
3. Case studies on warehouses implementing green initiatives. 72

Cybersecurity in Smart Warehousing 81
1. Importance of cybersecurity in connected warehouses. 81
2. Threats to smart warehouse systems and best practices for securing them. 81
3. Building a resilient smart warehouse infrastructure. 81

The Future of Smart Warehousing 90
1. Emerging technologies shaping the future: edge computing, blockchain, and 5G. 90
2. The potential impact of these technologies on warehouse operations. 90
3. Predictions and insights on the evolution of warehousing over the next decade. 90

Case Studies and Real-World Applications 99
1. In-depth case studies of successful smart warehouses across different industries. 99
2. Lessons learned from early adopters of smart warehouse technology. 99
3. Key takeaways for businesses considering the transition to a smart warehouse. 99

Implementing a Smart Warehouse: Step-by-Step Guide 108
1. Key considerations before transitioning to a smart warehouse. 108
2. Step-by-step approach to upgrading technology, training staff, and phasing in changes. 108
3. Budgeting, planning, and ROI analysis for smart warehouse implementation. 108

Challenges and Limitations in Smart Warehousing 117
1. Common challenges businesses face (cost, integration, training, maintenance). 117
2. Limitations of current smart technologies and how companies are overcoming them. 117
3. Addressing the human factor: workforce adaptation and training for new technologies. 117

Conclusion: Smart Warehousing as a Competitive Advantage 126
1. Recap of the benefits of smart warehousing. 126
2. How smart warehousing creates a competitive edge in logistics and supply chain management. 126
3. Encouraging the adoption of smart technology for future-ready warehouse management. 126

Additional Sections: 133
Glossary of Smart Warehousing Terms: Define key terms for readers new to the topic. 133
Resources: List of software, automation providers, and platforms for further learning. 133

Appendix: Templates, checklists, and assessment tools for smart warehouse readiness. 133

Introduction to Smart Warehousing

1. Overview of Smart Warehousing and Its Significance

Warehousing is a crucial component of modern supply chain management, serving as a central hub for storing, organizing, and managing inventory before it reaches the end customer. However, in the age of digital transformation, the warehouse itself has evolved from a simple storage facility into a sophisticated, technology-driven environment, often referred to as a "smart warehouse." A smart warehouse leverages a combination of cutting-edge technologies such as automation, artificial intelligence (AI), the Internet of Things (IoT), robotics, and data analytics to streamline operations, enhance accuracy, and increase efficiency.

Smart warehousing technology enables real-time inventory tracking, automated order picking, demand forecasting, and better resource management. The integration of these technologies has redefined the role of warehouses in the supply chain, transforming them from passive storage spaces to dynamic and responsive centers of operational intelligence. By automating repetitive tasks, improving accuracy in stock handling, and enabling faster response times, smart warehousing helps organizations stay competitive in a market where customer expectations for speed and accuracy are higher than ever.

In a smart warehouse, automated systems can manage a variety of tasks, from organizing stock to performing quality checks, making processes more efficient and cost-effective. For example, robotic arms may handle picking and packing, autonomous guided vehicles (AGVs) transport items across the warehouse, and drones assist in inventory checks. Additionally, IoT sensors monitor environmental factors to ensure proper storage conditions, and data analytics provide insights that enable continuous improvement. These innovations contribute to a well-coordinated warehouse where human labor is complemented and optimized by technology, significantly reducing the margin of error and enabling rapid response to fluctuating demand.

Smart warehousing is significant not only for operational efficiency but also for strategic competitiveness. As companies strive to reduce costs, increase agility, and deliver a seamless customer experience, the adoption of smart warehousing technologies offers an opportunity to differentiate themselves in a crowded market. It also represents a shift toward a data-driven supply chain, where insights gathered in the warehouse can impact broader decision-making in areas like procurement, production, and logistics.

2. Evolution of Warehouses: From Traditional to Digital and Automated Systems

The journey from traditional warehousing to today's smart warehouses reflects the broader trends of industrial innovation, particularly the recent surge in digital transformation. Let's explore how warehouses have evolved over time:

Traditional Warehouses

In traditional warehouses, processes were largely manual, involving significant human labor for tasks such as unloading, storing, picking, and packing. Inventory records were managed with paper or basic digital tools like spreadsheets, and tracking stock levels relied on regular physical inventory counts. While traditional warehouses could meet the basic storage needs of companies, they were labor-intensive, prone to human error, and lacked real-time inventory visibility, which limited responsiveness and efficiency.

Labor costs and space utilization were also major challenges in traditional warehouses. The manual processes meant that scaling up operations required hiring more workers, which increased costs and decreased efficiency. Space was often underutilized because inventory placement and retrieval were not optimized. Delays in order fulfillment and a lack of transparency in stock levels often resulted in poor customer service and inventory inaccuracies, leading to increased operating costs and dissatisfied customers.

Emergence of Digital Warehousing

As technology advanced, digital tools and systems began to transform warehouse management practices. The development of warehouse management systems (WMS) allowed companies to digitize their inventory records, improving accuracy and enabling more efficient tracking of stock levels. With WMS, companies could monitor stock levels, generate reports, and automate aspects of inventory management, leading to improved efficiency and accuracy.

Digital warehouses introduced barcode scanning and radio-frequency identification (RFID) technology, which allowed for faster and more accurate data capture, improving the speed and accuracy of stock management. With the advent of these technologies, employees could track inventory at a granular level, allowing for more precise forecasting and planning.

Digitalization laid the groundwork for automation, as it enabled more streamlined and standardized processes that could eventually be handed over to machines. Real-time tracking of stock movement, order fulfillment status, and inventory levels helped reduce delays and enhanced the reliability of data, which paved the way for predictive analytics in inventory management. The shift to digital warehousing marked a significant step forward, as it enabled the warehouse to become more responsive to the demands of the broader supply chain.

Rise of Automated and Smart Warehousing

With the introduction of advanced automation technologies, warehouses began to transition to smart, fully automated environments. Automated systems such as robotic picking arms, AGVs, drones, and conveyor systems drastically reduced the reliance on manual labor, allowing warehouses to scale up without significantly increasing headcount. By automating repetitive tasks such as sorting, picking, packing, and transporting goods, smart warehouses could operate around the clock, dramatically increasing throughput and reducing order fulfillment times.

Smart warehouses also integrate IoT devices, allowing for real-time monitoring of various factors, such as temperature, humidity, and stock movement. IoT-enabled sensors provide data that helps maintain optimal storage conditions for perishable items, improving quality control and reducing waste. Additionally, these sensors allow companies to monitor equipment health, enabling predictive maintenance that minimizes downtime and increases operational efficiency.

Machine learning and data analytics play a critical role in smart warehousing, helping companies forecast demand, optimize inventory levels, and adjust workflows in real time based on changing conditions. For example, AI-powered systems can predict order patterns and adjust inventory allocation based on forecasted demand, ensuring that the right products are available at the right time. Robotics further streamline operations, with automated storage and retrieval systems (AS/RS) handling high-density storage needs and enabling precise picking operations, which is particularly useful in e-commerce and industries with diverse SKUs.

The evolution toward smart warehousing is part of the broader trend of Industry 4.0, where data, connectivity, and automation drive operational efficiencies and enable new capabilities. This new generation of warehouses does not just store inventory; it contributes to a dynamic, data-driven supply chain that is responsive to market demands and resilient in the face of disruptions.

3. Why Businesses Are Investing in Smart Warehouses and the Key Benefits

As global supply chains grow more complex, businesses are investing in smart warehousing to stay competitive, increase efficiency, and meet rising customer expectations. Here are the primary benefits driving this investment:

a) Enhanced Efficiency and Productivity

One of the main benefits of smart warehousing is the significant boost in operational efficiency and productivity. Automation reduces the time needed for various tasks, from picking and packing to loading and dispatching. Smart warehouses can operate 24/7, maximizing output and ensuring faster order fulfillment. With robotics and AI-powered systems, companies can handle more orders per hour with fewer errors, increasing productivity without a proportional rise in labor costs.

Automated systems in smart warehouses also help reduce the idle time typically associated with manual labor. For example, AGVs transport goods across the warehouse more quickly and consistently than human workers, while robotic arms handle picking and packing without fatigue. This increase in productivity allows businesses to scale up operations to meet increased demand without the need for costly expansions.

b) Improved Accuracy and Reduced Errors

The integration of technologies such as barcode scanning, RFID, and AI reduces errors in inventory management, minimizing issues like stock discrepancies, misplaced items, and order inaccuracies. Smart warehousing enables real-time tracking and verification of inventory, ensuring that each item is accounted for accurately. This accuracy is crucial for maintaining customer satisfaction, as it reduces instances of late deliveries, wrong shipments, and stockouts.

Data analytics further enhance accuracy by identifying patterns and trends in demand, allowing companies to adjust their inventory levels and prevent overstocking or understocking. By reducing errors and improving inventory visibility, smart warehouses help companies avoid costly mistakes and provide a higher level of service to their customers.

c) Faster Order Fulfillment and Response Times

Smart warehouses are designed to meet the modern demands of e-commerce and fast shipping. With automated systems, companies can fulfill orders more quickly, improving response times and meeting customer expectations for rapid delivery. This speed is especially important in the era of same-day and next-day delivery services, where traditional warehouse operations often struggle to keep up.

Automation in picking, packing, and shipping processes means that orders can be processed as soon as they are received, reducing lead times and ensuring faster order dispatch. In high-demand periods, such as holiday seasons, this increased speed allows companies to handle higher order volumes without compromising on service quality.

d) Cost Savings and Improved ROI

While the initial investment in smart warehousing technology can be substantial, the long-term cost savings are significant. Automation reduces labor costs by minimizing the need for manual handling of goods, while predictive maintenance enabled by IoT sensors reduces equipment downtime and maintenance costs. Inventory optimization helps avoid overstocking, which reduces carrying costs and prevents losses due to expired or outdated stock.

By improving accuracy, reducing labor requirements, and increasing productivity, smart warehouses enable companies to achieve a higher return on investment (ROI). Additionally, many smart technologies are scalable, allowing businesses to expand operations with minimal additional costs, which further enhances the cost-effectiveness of these investments.

e) Enhanced Data Insights and Decision-Making

Smart warehouses generate vast amounts of data that can be analyzed to gain insights into operations and drive continuous improvement. Advanced analytics enable companies to track key performance indicators (KPIs) in real-time, such as order processing time, picking accuracy, and stock levels. This data helps identify areas for improvement, optimize workflows, and enhance resource allocation.

Machine learning algorithms can also be used to forecast demand, enabling proactive adjustments in inventory and staffing levels to align with anticipated sales trends. This data-driven approach leads to more informed decision-making and allows companies to be more responsive to changing market conditions.

f) Scalability and Flexibility

Smart warehouses are inherently more flexible and scalable than traditional warehouses. The modular nature of smart technology allows businesses to expand or adapt their operations as needed, whether by increasing storage capacity, adding new automation systems, or adjusting workflows. This scalability is essential for businesses experiencing seasonal demand spikes or rapid growth, as they can expand capacity without significant downtime or disruption.

By investing in smart warehousing, companies are not only improving their current operations but also future-proofing their supply chains. The flexibility of smart warehouses makes them well-suited to handle the challenges of an evolving marketplace, allowing businesses to scale their operations in line with customer demand.

Smart warehousing is transforming the traditional concept of warehousing by integrating advanced technology and automation. This transformation allows companies to maximize productivity, reduce costs, and respond swiftly to market demands. As more companies embrace this approach, smart warehouses are set to become the standard for efficient, data-driven supply chain operations, driving competitive advantage and setting new benchmarks in the industry.

Core Technologies in Smart Warehouses

- ❖ 1.Detailed overview of technologies powering smart warehouses: IoT, AI, machine learning, robotics, and big data.

- ❖ 2.How these technologies interact within a warehouse setting.

- ❖ 3.Examples of major companies leading the way in implementing these technologies.

1. Detailed Overview of Technologies Powering Smart Warehouses

Smart warehousing relies on a suite of advanced technologies that transform traditional storage facilities into efficient, data-driven ecosystems. Key technologies like the Internet of Things (IoT), Artificial Intelligence (AI), machine learning, robotics, and big data play a pivotal role in enabling automated, precise, and responsive warehouse management.

IoT (Internet of Things)

The Internet of Things (IoT) is foundational in smart warehousing. IoT refers to the network of physical devices, sensors, and machines that communicate and share data over the internet. In a warehouse setting, IoT sensors and devices monitor and manage everything from temperature and humidity to the movement of goods, enabling real-time data collection and analysis. By tracking inventory, asset locations, equipment status, and environmental conditions, IoT increases visibility and helps optimize space and inventory management.

For example, IoT sensors can track a product's journey from the moment it arrives at the warehouse until it leaves for shipment, reducing the risk of misplaced items. Furthermore, IoT sensors monitor equipment health, predicting potential breakdowns and enabling proactive maintenance to prevent operational disruptions.

Artificial Intelligence (AI)

Artificial Intelligence (AI) is the engine behind many smart warehouse applications, allowing for enhanced decision-making and operational efficiency. AI algorithms analyze vast amounts of data generated by IoT devices, warehouse management systems (WMS), and enterprise resource planning (ERP) systems to optimize workflows, forecast demand, and automate decision-making.

In smart warehouses, AI-powered systems handle predictive analytics for demand forecasting, ensuring that inventory levels align with expected sales. AI also improves picking and packing accuracy by predicting the most efficient paths and methods, reducing labor costs and minimizing errors. AI algorithms can even monitor supply chain conditions outside the warehouse, adjusting inventory levels and labor allocations in response to changes in demand, supplier delays, or transportation issues.

Machine Learning

Machine learning, a subset of AI, further enhances smart warehousing by enabling systems to learn from data and improve over time. Machine learning algorithms analyze historical data to identify patterns and trends, allowing the warehouse to adapt to shifting demands. For example, machine learning models can analyze order histories to predict which products are most likely to be ordered during specific times, allowing for dynamic stocking and improved space utilization.

Machine learning is also used in image recognition for automated quality control. By analyzing images captured by cameras, machine learning models can identify defects or damages in goods and alert warehouse staff to potential issues before they affect the customer.

Robotics

Robotics play a transformative role in reducing manual labor, increasing speed, and enhancing accuracy in smart warehouses. Automated Guided Vehicles (AGVs), Automated Mobile Robots (AMRs), and robotic arms perform various functions, from picking and packing to transporting goods and stocking shelves. AGVs and AMRs use sensors and AI to navigate warehouse floors autonomously, transporting items from storage locations to packing stations.

Collaborative robots, or "cobots," work alongside human employees, handling repetitive tasks like lifting and transporting heavy items, which reduces the physical strain on workers and increases productivity. Robotic picking systems are particularly useful in e-commerce, where they can rapidly locate, retrieve, and pack items for orders with minimal human intervention.

Big Data and Data Analytics

Big data enables smart warehouses to analyze the massive volumes of data generated by IoT devices, AI systems, and other warehouse technologies. By collecting and analyzing data on inventory levels, equipment health, employee productivity, and order fulfillment rates, smart warehouses can identify inefficiencies and make data-driven improvements. Data analytics enables predictive maintenance, demand forecasting, inventory optimization, and real-time performance monitoring.

Big data analytics also aids in uncovering long-term trends and optimizing workflows. For instance, data from previous seasons helps warehouses prepare for peak demand periods, while analysis of employee movement patterns can help optimize layout to reduce travel time and increase productivity.

2. How These Technologies Interact Within a Warehouse Setting

The interaction between IoT, AI, machine learning, robotics, and big data enables seamless, efficient, and highly coordinated warehouse operations. Here's how these technologies work together:

IoT and Data Collection

IoT sensors and devices gather real-time data on various parameters, such as inventory levels, environmental conditions, and equipment status. This data is then transmitted to a central system, where it can be processed by AI algorithms for decision-making and optimization.

For instance, an IoT-enabled smart shelf may detect low stock levels of a specific item and send an alert to the warehouse management system (WMS). The WMS then uses machine learning algorithms to forecast future demand for that item, determining the optimal restocking levels and timings.

AI and Machine Learning for Optimization

AI and machine learning analyze the data collected by IoT devices to identify patterns, predict future demands, and optimize operations. For example, AI can determine the most efficient picking routes based on order volumes and item locations, while machine learning models predict order patterns and adjust stock levels in anticipation of peak demand.

In a smart warehouse, AI systems can dynamically adjust workflows based on real-time data. If an IoT sensor detects that a conveyor belt is operating at a reduced speed, the AI system might reroute picking tasks to ensure that the delay does not impact overall throughput.

Robotics and Automation

Robots in a smart warehouse execute tasks autonomously, following instructions from the AI-driven WMS. When an order is placed, AI determines the most efficient picking and packing path, instructing AGVs or AMRs to retrieve items. The robots then transport the items to a packing station, where robotic arms handle sorting and packing.

These interactions minimize human involvement in physically demanding tasks, enabling employees to focus on more strategic, value-added activities. The integration of robotics with AI and IoT also improves safety, as robots can be equipped with sensors to avoid obstacles and adjust their speed based on surrounding conditions.

Big Data Analytics and Decision Support

Big data analytics enhances decision-making by providing a comprehensive overview of warehouse operations. Data collected from IoT sensors, robotic movements, and AI-optimized workflows is analyzed to provide insights into performance trends and areas for improvement. For instance, analytics might reveal bottlenecks in the picking process, prompting the warehouse manager to reconfigure the layout or deploy additional resources.

By leveraging big data, smart warehouses can implement continuous improvement, enhancing efficiency, accuracy, and customer satisfaction over time. The data-driven insights also support strategic planning, enabling warehouse managers to make informed decisions about resource allocation, inventory management, and labor planning.

3. Examples of Major Companies Leading the Way in Implementing These Technologies

Several companies are at the forefront of implementing smart warehouse technologies, setting new benchmarks for efficiency and customer satisfaction. Here are some of the major players in this space:

Amazon

Amazon has led the way in smart warehousing with its extensive use of robotics, AI, and IoT. Amazon's warehouses use thousands of Kiva robots, which autonomously transport shelves of products to human pickers, reducing the time needed for order fulfillment. The company's AI-driven algorithms optimize picking routes and predict demand trends, ensuring that inventory is replenished efficiently. IoT sensors monitor equipment and environmental conditions, supporting a seamless flow of goods from stocking to shipping. Amazon's commitment to innovation in warehousing has enabled it to offer same-day and next-day delivery options, setting a high standard in the e-commerce industry.

Walmart

Walmart has also embraced smart warehousing, investing in AI and robotics to streamline its supply chain. Walmart uses robotics for tasks like scanning shelves, inventory management, and order picking. The company's AI-driven systems optimize inventory levels based on demand forecasts, ensuring that products are always in stock. Walmart has also deployed drones in some of its warehouses for rapid inventory checks, improving accuracy and reducing labor costs. Through these investments, Walmart has enhanced efficiency and reduced order fulfillment times, helping it compete effectively in the retail market.

Alibaba

Alibaba, the Chinese e-commerce giant, has implemented smart warehousing across its logistics network. The company's Cainiao Smart Logistics Network relies on robotics and AI to handle high volumes of orders during peak periods like Singles' Day. Alibaba's warehouses use AGVs to transport goods, and AI-powered systems optimize workflows, reducing human error and speeding up order fulfillment. Cainiao's smart warehouses leverage IoT and data analytics to monitor inventory in real time, adjusting operations based on demand patterns. This approach has enabled Alibaba to process millions of orders quickly and accurately, reinforcing its position as a leader in global e-commerce.

DHL

Global logistics provider DHL has been a pioneer in adopting smart warehousing solutions across its facilities worldwide. The company uses robotic systems for picking, packing, and sorting tasks, which improves accuracy and reduces lead times. DHL also employs AI for route optimization and demand forecasting, allowing it to manage its global inventory effectively. IoT devices and big data analytics are integrated into DHL's warehouses to monitor assets, track shipments, and predict equipment maintenance needs. This data-driven approach enhances DHL's efficiency and strengthens its reputation as a leader in logistics and supply chain innovation.

Siemens

Siemens, a global industrial technology company, has implemented smart warehousing at its manufacturing sites to support its Industry 4.0 initiatives. Siemens' warehouses utilize a combination of robotics, IoT, and AI to manage raw materials and finished goods. AGVs transport items within the warehouse, while IoT sensors track inventory levels and equipment status. AI algorithms optimize workflows based on real-time data, reducing operational costs and increasing throughput. Siemens' smart warehousing approach is aligned with its broader commitment to digital transformation, helping it meet the demands of its customers and remain competitive in a rapidly evolving market.

Smart warehouses represent the future of logistics and supply chain management, combining IoT, AI, machine learning, robotics, and big data to create a highly efficient, accurate, and responsive operational environment. By leveraging these technologies, leading companies are redefining the standards of warehousing, enabling faster, more reliable order fulfillment, and setting the stage for even more advanced logistics solutions in the years to come.

Warehouse Management Systems (WMS) and Smart Warehouse Software

- ❖ 1. Role of WMS in smart warehousing.

- ❖ 2. How WMS integrates with smart technology (IoT, AI, etc.) to enhance efficiency.

- ❖ 3. Key features of a smart WMS and selection considerations for businesses.

Here's a detailed look at Warehouse Management Systems (WMS) and Smart Warehouse Software, covering their role in smart warehousing, integration with emerging technologies, and important features to consider when selecting a WMS.

Warehouse Management Systems (WMS) and Smart Warehouse Software

1. Role of WMS in Smart Warehousing

In the evolution of smart warehousing, a Warehouse Management System (WMS) is crucial. WMS is a software solution designed to manage, control, and optimize warehouse operations, from inventory tracking to order fulfillment. In a smart warehouse, WMS acts as the central hub, coordinating various activities and leveraging automation, data analysis, and connectivity to improve productivity and efficiency.

Key roles of WMS in smart warehousing include:

Inventory Management: A WMS offers real-time visibility into stock levels, locations, and movements, which helps reduce errors, prevent stockouts, and improve inventory accuracy. By managing stock across multiple locations and warehouses, WMS ensures that inventory is optimized and readily available.

Order Fulfillment: WMS improves the speed and accuracy of order fulfillment by coordinating picking, packing, and shipping. It directs workers or robots to specific locations, ensuring items are picked correctly, packaged appropriately, and dispatched on time.

Labor Management: By tracking employee productivity and assigning tasks based on workload and availability, WMS helps maximize labor efficiency. In smart warehouses with robotic systems, WMS also oversees robot allocation and performance, balancing tasks between human and robotic workers.

Performance Analytics: With robust data collection and analytics, WMS provides insights into key performance indicators (KPIs) such as order accuracy, inventory turnover, and picking speed. These metrics allow warehouse managers to identify areas for improvement and streamline operations.

Cost Reduction: By reducing labor costs, improving inventory accuracy, and optimizing space utilization, a WMS helps decrease operational costs, contributing to overall cost-effectiveness.

2. How WMS Integrates with Smart Technology (IoT, AI, etc.) to Enhance Efficiency

A WMS integrates seamlessly with smart technologies like IoT, AI, machine learning, and robotics, enhancing warehouse efficiency and enabling smarter, data-driven decision-making.

IoT Integration

IoT devices, such as sensors, RFID tags, and smart shelves, are integral to a smart warehouse and connect with WMS to provide real-time data. This IoT-WMS integration allows continuous tracking of inventory, assets, and environmental conditions, giving warehouse managers accurate and up-to-date information. For example:

Automated Inventory Tracking: IoT-enabled RFID tags and barcode scanners allow WMS to automatically log item movements, updating inventory levels in real time.

Environmental Monitoring: Sensors track temperature, humidity, and other environmental factors, with WMS setting automated alerts when certain thresholds are exceeded, ensuring safe storage conditions.

Asset Management: IoT sensors track the location and usage of warehouse equipment, helping WMS allocate resources more effectively and schedule maintenance.

AI and Machine Learning Integration

AI and machine learning algorithms within WMS analyze historical and real-time data to optimize workflows, predict demand patterns, and manage inventory levels. This integration is particularly useful for demand forecasting, route optimization, and operational planning.

Predictive Analytics: WMS uses AI-driven predictive analytics to forecast inventory needs, ensuring the right amount of stock is maintained. This is especially valuable for seasonal businesses or those with fluctuating demand patterns.

Route Optimization: AI algorithms within WMS calculate the most efficient picking and packing routes, reducing the distance traveled by pickers and robots, saving time, and minimizing labor costs.

Dynamic Slotting: Machine learning models analyze item demand and optimize storage locations based on access frequency. By positioning high-demand items closer to picking areas, WMS reduces pick times, increasing order fulfillment speed.

Robotics and Automation Integration

Robotics integration allows WMS to assign and monitor tasks for robotic systems like Automated Guided Vehicles (AGVs), Automated Mobile Robots (AMRs), and robotic arms.

Automated Picking and Packing: WMS directs robots to retrieve, transport, and pack items, streamlining the order fulfillment process. Robots work alongside human workers or independently, depending on warehouse layout and tasks.

Automated Material Handling: WMS coordinates with AGVs and AMRs for material transport, ensuring items move through the warehouse efficiently without human intervention.

Collaborative Workflows: WMS assigns robots to support tasks that are repetitive or physically strenuous, while human workers handle more complex or high-value tasks, resulting in efficient, collaborative workflows.

Big Data and Analytics Integration

WMS leverages big data to track, analyze, and report on various warehouse functions. The integration of big data analytics enables a WMS to provide actionable insights for better decision-making.

Performance Analysis: By analyzing data on order fulfillment, picking accuracy, and labor productivity, WMS identifies bottlenecks and areas for improvement.

Cost Optimization: WMS analyzes cost data across labor, inventory, and equipment, providing insights to reduce operational costs and enhance profitability.

Strategic Planning: WMS uses data trends to guide long-term planning, helping warehouses plan for peak seasons, scale operations, or invest in new technologies.

3. Key Features of a Smart WMS and Selection Considerations for Businesses

A smart WMS offers several advanced features designed to support automation, data-driven management, and efficient workflow coordination. When selecting a WMS, businesses should consider these core features and evaluate them based on their unique needs and goals.

Key Features of a Smart WMS

Real-Time Inventory Tracking

A smart WMS should support real-time inventory visibility, allowing managers to track stock levels and item locations instantaneously. This feature helps prevent stockouts, reduces overstocking, and enhances order accuracy.

Automated Order Fulfillment

Automated order fulfillment processes, such as pick-path optimization, robotic picking, and automated sorting, reduce human labor requirements and enhance order accuracy and speed.

Integration Capabilities

A smart WMS must integrate with various warehouse technologies like IoT, robotics, and other software platforms (e.g., ERP, CRM). These integrations enable a unified system that operates efficiently and shares data across the organization.

Data Analytics and Reporting

Advanced reporting and analytics tools help warehouse managers understand KPIs, monitor performance, and identify opportunities for process improvements. Predictive analytics are also beneficial for demand forecasting and inventory planning.

Scalability and Flexibility

A scalable WMS grows with the business, allowing for new modules or features as operations expand. Scalability is essential for businesses planning to introduce more automation or increase storage capacity in the future.

Mobile Access and User-Friendly Interface

Mobile access enables warehouse staff to use tablets or smartphones to interact with the WMS on the go, while a user-friendly interface minimizes training time and enhances operational efficiency.

Labor and Task Management

A smart WMS should allocate tasks to human or robotic workers based on workload and skill, track productivity, and monitor task completion rates. This feature is crucial for optimizing labor resources and managing peak times effectively.

Automated Alerts and Notifications

Automated alerts notify managers of critical events such as low stock levels, equipment malfunctions, or delayed orders. This proactive feature allows issues to be addressed quickly, minimizing disruptions.

Selection Considerations for Businesses

When choosing a WMS, businesses should assess their specific operational requirements, growth plans, and technology preferences. Here are some factors to consider:

Integration with Existing Systems: Ensure the WMS can integrate with your current ERP, CRM, IoT devices, and other software platforms. A WMS that seamlessly connects with these systems will streamline operations and improve data sharing.

Customization Options: Choose a WMS that offers customizable workflows, reports, and interfaces. Customization allows the system to be tailored to unique operational needs, making it easier to implement and maximizing its value.

Scalability for Future Growth: Select a WMS that can scale with your business. Scalable WMS solutions can accommodate future automation, additional storage, or expanded facilities without significant adjustments or replacement costs.

Ease of Implementation and Training: The WMS should have a user-friendly interface and provide training resources or support. Systems that are easy to implement and learn reduce downtime and help staff adapt quickly.

Vendor Support and Reliability: Choose a WMS vendor with a strong reputation for support and system reliability. Responsive vendor support is essential for addressing any technical issues that may arise.

Cost-Benefit Analysis: While some WMS solutions may have higher upfront costs, consider the potential ROI from efficiency improvements, labor savings, and enhanced accuracy. Evaluate the total cost of ownership, including licensing, maintenance, and upgrade fees.

A smart WMS is a critical component of a smart warehouse, providing the functionality needed to manage inventory, orders, and labor with precision. By integrating with IoT, AI, robotics, and big data, a WMS enables a warehouse to operate at optimal efficiency, providing real-time insights and adaptive workflows that align with modern business demands. Businesses that carefully evaluate their needs and select the right WMS can significantly enhance their operational agility, reduce costs, and improve customer satisfaction.

Automation in Warehousing: Robots, Drones, and AGVs

- ❖ ***1.Types of warehouse automation: robotic arms, automated*** *guided vehicles (AGVs), drones, and autonomous forklifts.*

- ❖ *2.Advantages of using robotics and automation in warehouses.*

- ❖ *3.Case studies on companies successfully implementing robotics.*

Automation in Warehousing: Robots, Drones, and AGVs

1. Types of Warehouse Automation: Robotic Arms, Automated Guided Vehicles (AGVs), Drones, and Autonomous Forklifts

Warehouse automation encompasses a range of technologies designed to streamline operations, reduce human error, and maximize efficiency. Some of the most prominent automation tools in warehouses today include robotic arms, AGVs, drones, and autonomous forklifts. Each of these tools serves unique roles in enhancing operational efficiency and reducing costs.

Robotic Arms

Robotic arms are highly versatile and precise devices used for repetitive tasks in warehousing, such as picking, packing, palletizing, and sorting. Equipped with advanced sensors and programming, robotic arms can handle a wide range of items, from delicate goods to heavy boxes.

Picking and Sorting: Robotic arms equipped with machine vision systems can accurately pick items based on size, weight, and shape, reducing the need for manual handling.

Palletizing and Depalletizing: Robotic arms can efficiently load and unload items from pallets, enhancing speed and consistency in stacking patterns.

Packaging and Assembly: Robotic arms help automate packaging and product assembly, handling fragile or complex items without damaging them.

Automated Guided Vehicles (AGVs)

AGVs are self-guided vehicles used to transport goods within the warehouse. They follow a fixed path, often using magnetic strips, sensors, or predefined routes to move items between designated areas.

Material Transport: AGVs move raw materials, finished products, and packaging supplies from one area to another, minimizing manual handling.

Inventory Replenishment: AGVs can automatically restock shelves or move goods from storage to picking areas, streamlining order fulfillment.

Forklift Replacement: In some warehouses, AGVs are used in place of forklifts, reducing the need for human operators and lowering accident risks.

Drones

Drones in warehousing provide an aerial solution to inventory management and inspections. Equipped with cameras and sensors, drones can scan barcodes, track stock levels, and even monitor environmental conditions.

Inventory Scanning: Drones fly through warehouse aisles, scanning barcodes and updating inventory records in real time, especially useful in large warehouses with high ceilings.

Environmental Monitoring: Some drones are equipped with thermal or humidity sensors to monitor temperature-sensitive items and alert managers of potential risks.

Surveillance and Security: Drones patrol the warehouse, providing security and detecting any unusual activities or unauthorized access.

Autonomous Forklifts

Autonomous forklifts function similarly to AGVs but with greater lifting and stacking capabilities. These vehicles navigate complex paths, retrieve or store pallets on high shelves, and assist in loading and unloading operations.

Heavy Load Management: Autonomous forklifts handle heavy goods, reducing the need for manual operation and enhancing safety.

Precision Stacking: They are equipped with sensors to ensure precise stacking and prevent product damage, which is especially useful in high-density storage areas.

Flexible Navigation: Unlike traditional AGVs, autonomous forklifts use machine learning to navigate complex environments, making them suitable for dynamic warehouses where paths may change.

2. Advantages of Using Robotics and Automation in Warehouses

Implementing robotics and automation in warehouses offers significant benefits that enhance efficiency, reduce costs, and improve workplace safety. Here are some of the primary advantages:

Increased Productivity

Automation accelerates routine processes like picking, packing, and transporting goods, allowing warehouses to handle higher volumes in shorter times. Automated systems operate continuously without breaks, fatigue, or errors, increasing throughput and reducing order cycle times.

Improved Accuracy and Consistency

Robots and automated systems perform repetitive tasks with precision, reducing human errors in picking and inventory management. This accuracy minimizes costly mistakes, such as incorrect shipments or misplaced items, improving customer satisfaction and reducing return rates.

Enhanced Safety

Automation reduces the need for human involvement in potentially dangerous tasks like heavy lifting, operating forklifts, or working at height. With robotic systems handling these tasks, warehouses can minimize workplace accidents and create a safer environment for employees.

Optimized Space Utilization

Robots and AGVs can operate in tight spaces and narrow aisles, allowing warehouses to optimize their layout and increase storage density. With automated stacking systems, warehouses can store goods in high racks or densely packed areas, maximizing floor space and reducing the need for expansion.

Real-Time Data Collection and Analysis

Automation systems collect vast amounts of data on inventory levels, equipment status, and task completion times. With real-time data analytics, warehouse managers gain valuable insights into performance, enabling better forecasting, planning, and resource allocation.

Cost Savings

Although implementing robotics requires upfront investment, automation reduces long-term labor costs, minimizes product damage, and improves operational efficiency, resulting in substantial cost savings over time.

3. Case Studies on Companies Successfully Implementing Robotics

Many companies are leveraging robotics and automation to enhance their warehouse operations. Below are case studies of three major companies successfully implementing warehouse automation.

Case Study 1: Amazon – Robotic Arms and AGVs for High-Speed Fulfillment

Amazon is one of the most well-known examples of a company using robotics in its fulfillment centers. In 2012, Amazon acquired Kiva Systems (now known as Amazon Robotics) to streamline its warehouse operations with robotic technology. Today, Amazon's warehouses use over 500,000 robots, including robotic arms and AGVs, to support its rapid fulfillment processes.

AGVs for Inventory Movement: Amazon uses AGVs to move shelves of products directly to human workers. This reduces the time workers spend walking around the warehouse, allowing for faster order processing.

Robotic Arms for Sorting: In its larger fulfillment centers, Amazon deploys robotic arms for sorting, packaging, and handling heavy items, reducing the risk of injury and ensuring consistent, accurate order fulfillment.

Enhanced Speed and Accuracy: By integrating robotics, Amazon can fulfill orders in as little as two hours, especially in urban areas with high demand. Robotics also contribute to Amazon's high accuracy rate, reducing order errors and improving customer satisfaction.

Case Study 2: DHL – Drones and Collaborative Robots (Cobots) for Improved Efficiency

DHL has been a pioneer in experimenting with different forms of warehouse automation, including drones and collaborative robots. In its Innovation Center in Germany, DHL tests and deploys cutting-edge technology to improve logistics and warehousing efficiency.

Drones for Inventory Management: DHL uses drones to perform inventory scanning and cycle counting in its larger warehouses. The drones scan barcodes on high shelves and provide real-time data on stock levels, significantly reducing the time and labor required for inventory management.

Collaborative Robots for Picking: DHL has deployed cobots that work alongside human workers in picking operations. These robots assist workers by fetching items, handling heavy loads, and moving goods from picking areas to packing stations.

Increased Productivity: By integrating drones and cobots, DHL has reduced the time spent on manual inventory checks by 80%, allowing workers to focus on more complex tasks and increasing overall productivity.

Case Study 3: Walmart – Autonomous Forklifts and AI-Driven Systems

Walmart, a retail giant with an extensive logistics network, has implemented autonomous forklifts and AI-driven systems in its distribution centers to streamline operations and improve accuracy.

Autonomous Forklifts for Pallet Management: Walmart's autonomous forklifts manage pallet movement, transporting items between storage areas, and loading docks without human intervention. This reduces labor requirements and minimizes risks associated with manual forklift operation.

AI-Driven Sorting Systems: Walmart employs AI algorithms to improve sorting efficiency, grouping items based on destination, size, and weight to optimize loading processes.

Improved Efficiency and Reduced Costs: By deploying autonomous forklifts and AI-driven systems, Walmart has reduced its labor costs and increased the speed of its logistics network, helping the company keep up with high customer demand.

In summary, warehouse automation through robotic arms, AGVs, drones, and autonomous forklifts has transformed traditional warehousing into a highly efficient, precise, and scalable operation. From reducing labor costs to enhancing accuracy and ensuring worker safety, automation brings a wealth of benefits that enable businesses to meet growing consumer expectations and stay competitive in the marketplace.

Internet of Things (IoT) in Warehouse Management

❖ *1.How IoT enables smart inventory tracking, real-time data, and condition monitoring.*

❖ *2.Impact of IoT on asset tracking, environmental monitoring, and equipment maintenance.*

❖ *3.Security concerns and data privacy in IoT-enabled warehouses.*

1. How IoT Enables Smart Inventory Tracking, Real-Time Data, and Condition Monitoring

The Internet of Things (IoT) has revolutionized warehouse management by enabling connected devices to share data in real time, streamlining operations and boosting efficiency. IoT-driven smart warehouses are equipped with sensors, RFID tags, and IoT-enabled devices, creating a networked environment where managers can monitor and control inventory, track asset locations, and maintain optimal conditions.

Smart Inventory Tracking

In IoT-enabled warehouses, sensors and RFID tags attached to inventory items communicate with IoT platforms, providing detailed, real-time data on inventory levels, location, and movement. This transparency enables warehouse managers to reduce stockouts, streamline replenishment, and maintain optimal stock levels, all while minimizing human intervention.

Automated Inventory Counts: IoT devices can perform regular inventory checks autonomously, reducing the need for manual counts and ensuring accurate data. This helps minimize shrinkage and errors, especially in large warehouses.

Real-Time Inventory Visibility: By connecting inventory to the cloud, IoT allows managers and even customers to track inventory status and availability in real time, facilitating better decision-making and demand forecasting.

Real-Time Data and Analytics

The real-time data provided by IoT devices enhances visibility across the supply chain, enabling warehouses to analyze trends, identify inefficiencies, and optimize operations. IoT sensors track various aspects, such as inventory turnover, shelf life, and demand fluctuations, allowing managers to make data-driven decisions.

Demand Forecasting and Stock Optimization: IoT-generated data helps warehouses forecast demand accurately, preventing overstocking or understocking. Real-time data on inventory movement informs better stock replenishment strategies, reducing excess and minimizing waste.

Enhanced Process Monitoring: IoT devices enable continuous monitoring of all warehouse processes, including picking, packing, and shipping, providing actionable insights to refine workflows and improve service quality.

Condition Monitoring

IoT also enables condition monitoring by using sensors to track environmental factors, such as temperature, humidity, and light levels. Condition monitoring is essential for managing sensitive or perishable items like food, pharmaceuticals, and chemicals, ensuring they are stored under optimal conditions.

Temperature-Controlled Inventory: IoT sensors continuously monitor temperature-sensitive items, sending alerts if conditions deviate from safe ranges. This protects products from spoilage, improves quality control, and reduces losses.

Proactive Problem Resolution: With IoT, managers can detect potential issues in storage conditions early on, allowing for quick adjustments that maintain product integrity and prevent costly damage.

2. Impact of IoT on Asset Tracking, Environmental Monitoring, and Equipment Maintenance

Beyond inventory management, IoT devices enhance warehouse operations through improved asset tracking, environmental monitoring, and predictive equipment maintenance.

Asset Tracking

IoT-enabled asset tracking systems allow warehouses to monitor the location and status of valuable assets, such as equipment, vehicles, and storage containers. By attaching RFID tags or GPS devices to assets, warehouses gain real-time visibility into their location and usage.

Efficient Resource Allocation: IoT tracking ensures that assets are in the right place at the right time, minimizing delays and optimizing asset utilization.

Reduced Loss and Theft: Asset tracking reduces the risk of loss or theft by allowing managers to monitor assets' real-time locations. Alerts are triggered if assets move outside designated areas, enhancing security.

Seamless Logistics Coordination: By monitoring asset movement within the warehouse, IoT-enabled asset tracking facilitates seamless coordination between departments, reducing downtime and enhancing efficiency.

Environmental Monitoring

Environmental monitoring using IoT sensors helps warehouses maintain ideal conditions for various types of inventory. IoT sensors continuously measure temperature, humidity, light, and air quality, ensuring that storage environments remain within safe ranges.

Quality Assurance for Sensitive Goods: For items such as pharmaceuticals or perishables, environmental monitoring ensures that conditions meet regulatory requirements, reducing spoilage and maintaining quality.

Efficient Space Utilization: IoT-enabled sensors allow warehouses to allocate storage spaces based on product-specific needs, such as temperature-controlled areas, ensuring efficient use of space.

Automated Adjustments and Alerts: IoT systems can be programmed to adjust environmental conditions automatically. For example, if humidity levels rise, IoT devices can trigger dehumidifiers or alert personnel to intervene, preserving inventory quality.

Equipment Maintenance

IoT devices play a crucial role in equipment maintenance, enabling predictive and preventive maintenance by monitoring machinery performance in real time. This reduces equipment downtime, extends machinery life, and minimizes costly repairs.

Predictive Maintenance: IoT sensors collect data on equipment performance, detecting any signs of wear, overheating, or malfunctions. This information allows maintenance teams to schedule repairs before issues escalate, reducing unplanned downtime.

Reduced Operational Costs: By preventing unexpected breakdowns, predictive maintenance lowers repair costs and maximizes equipment uptime, ultimately contributing to operational efficiency.

Longer Equipment Lifespan: Continuous monitoring enables timely maintenance, extending the lifespan of critical warehouse machinery like forklifts, conveyors, and automated guided vehicles (AGVs).

3. Security Concerns and Data Privacy in IoT-Enabled Warehouses

With IoT transforming warehouse management, security and data privacy have become key concerns. IoT-enabled warehouses collect vast amounts of data on inventory, assets, equipment, and environmental conditions, creating potential vulnerabilities. Ensuring secure IoT deployment is essential to protect sensitive information and maintain trust with stakeholders.

Data Privacy Challenges

IoT devices collect data continuously, often including sensitive information such as inventory details, customer data, and asset locations. This data needs protection to avoid unauthorized access, data breaches, and misuse.

Data Encryption: Encrypting data from IoT devices ensures that information is secure both in transit and at rest, reducing the risk of unauthorized access.

Anonymization and Access Control: Limiting access to sensitive data and anonymizing personal information helps warehouses comply with data privacy regulations, such as GDPR, and safeguards customer trust.

Network Security Risks

IoT devices rely on wireless networks for communication, making them susceptible to cyberattacks, such as data interception, malware injection, or unauthorized access to the warehouse's network.

Securing IoT Devices: Ensuring that all IoT devices are password-protected and regularly updated with security patches reduces vulnerabilities. Firewalls and intrusion detection systems add an extra layer of protection.

Network Segmentation: Isolating IoT devices from the main warehouse network limits exposure in case of a breach, ensuring attackers cannot access other critical systems and data.

Device Management and Update Challenges

With large numbers of IoT devices deployed across warehouses, managing and updating these devices is challenging but crucial for security.

Remote Device Management: Using IoT management platforms, warehouses can monitor device performance, apply software updates, and enforce security protocols remotely, ensuring all devices stay secure and functional.

Regular Firmware Updates: Firmware updates often contain security patches that address new vulnerabilities. Ensuring IoT devices receive timely updates minimizes the risk of security breaches.

Employee Training on IoT Security

Warehouse employees interact with IoT devices daily, making it essential to train them on security best practices, such as handling sensitive data and recognizing suspicious activity.

Security Awareness Programs: Educating employees on IoT security, data privacy, and recognizing cyber threats enhances overall security and prevents accidental data exposure.

Access Controls and Authorization: Implementing role-based access ensures that only authorized personnel can access sensitive IoT systems and data, reducing the risk of internal breaches.

The Internet of Things has significantly enhanced warehouse management by providing real-time inventory tracking, environmental monitoring, and predictive maintenance. Through connected devices, warehouses can automate operations, optimize workflows, and improve data-driven decision-making. However, with these advancements come challenges related to data privacy and security. By prioritizing strong security measures, such as encryption, network segmentation, and employee training, warehouses can fully leverage the benefits of IoT while protecting their valuable data and assets.

Artificial Intelligence and Data Analytics for Smart Warehouses

- ❖ *1.Role of AI in demand forecasting, inventory optimization, and workflow automation.*

- ❖ *2.How predictive analytics improve decision-making and operational efficiency.*

- ❖ *3.Use of AI-powered cameras and sensors for quality control and anomaly detection.*

Artificial Intelligence and Data Analytics for Smart Warehouses

Artificial intelligence (AI) and data analytics are transforming warehouse management by providing advanced capabilities in demand forecasting, inventory optimization, workflow automation, and quality control. As warehouses adopt AI-driven systems, they achieve higher operational efficiency, better decision-making, and improved product quality.

1. Role of AI in Demand Forecasting, Inventory Optimization, and Workflow Automation

AI plays a pivotal role in making warehouses "smarter" by accurately forecasting demand, optimizing inventory levels, and automating workflows, leading to substantial cost savings and improved customer satisfaction.

Demand Forecasting

Traditional demand forecasting methods often rely on historical sales data and basic statistical methods, which can be limited in accuracy. In contrast, AI-driven forecasting models consider multiple data sources, including historical sales, current market trends, seasonal fluctuations, and even external factors such as economic indicators and weather conditions. AI algorithms can process this data to predict demand patterns more accurately, allowing warehouses to adjust stock levels proactively.

Reduced Stockouts and Overstocking: With accurate demand forecasts, warehouses can stock the right products in the right quantities, reducing the risks of stockouts or excess inventory.

Enhanced Customer Satisfaction: By maintaining optimal stock levels, AI-powered forecasting ensures that products are readily available, improving customer service and reducing delays.

Inventory Optimization

AI algorithms optimize inventory levels by analyzing real-time data on stock movement, storage capacity, and demand variability. Machine learning models continuously adapt based on new data, adjusting inventory levels dynamically to meet demand without overburdening storage resources.

Just-in-Time Inventory: AI-driven systems enable just-in-time (JIT) inventory practices by maintaining precise control over stock levels, allowing warehouses to minimize holding costs and improve cash flow.

Safety Stock Management: AI optimizes safety stock levels by considering historical variability, lead times, and demand uncertainty, ensuring that warehouses maintain enough buffer stock to meet unexpected demand without tying up excess capital.

Workflow Automation

AI also enhances workflow automation, from order processing to picking and packing. AI algorithms streamline warehouse operations by analyzing process flows and identifying areas for improvement. Robotic process automation (RPA) and machine learning models help automate repetitive tasks, reducing manual intervention.

Task Prioritization: AI can allocate tasks efficiently by prioritizing orders based on factors like shipping deadlines, inventory availability, and labor resources, ensuring that high-priority tasks are completed on time.

Labor Optimization: AI analyzes workforce productivity and shift patterns, optimizing labor deployment to match peak demand periods, reducing bottlenecks, and maximizing resource utilization.

2. How Predictive Analytics Improve Decision-Making and Operational Efficiency

Predictive analytics is a powerful tool in smart warehouses, enabling proactive decision-making by providing insights into future trends and operational needs. By leveraging AI-driven data analysis, predictive analytics transforms raw data into actionable insights, helping warehouses improve planning and operational efficiency.

Enhanced Decision-Making

Predictive analytics uses historical data, real-time inputs, and AI algorithms to predict future scenarios, providing warehouse managers with data-backed recommendations. For example, predictive models can analyze patterns in order frequency, seasonal demand spikes, and customer purchasing trends, helping managers make informed decisions regarding inventory allocation, staffing, and resource planning.

Proactive Issue Resolution: By forecasting potential issues, such as stock shortages or equipment malfunctions, predictive analytics allows managers to address them before they disrupt operations, ensuring smooth workflows.

Improved Supply Chain Coordination: Predictive analytics improves coordination across the supply chain by anticipating demand changes, adjusting production schedules, and aligning transportation plans, ultimately reducing lead times and enhancing customer satisfaction.

Operational Efficiency

Predictive analytics enhances operational efficiency by providing insights into optimal stock levels, space utilization, and resource allocation. For instance, by predicting peak demand periods, warehouses can adjust inventory levels and labor allocation in advance, minimizing stockouts and avoiding last-minute labor shortages.

Space Utilization Optimization: By analyzing past storage patterns and demand fluctuations, predictive analytics helps warehouses allocate storage space effectively, minimizing wasted space and improving accessibility for high-demand items.

Reduced Downtime through Predictive Maintenance: Predictive analytics monitors equipment performance data to predict potential breakdowns, enabling proactive maintenance that reduces downtime and extends equipment lifespan.

Dynamic Route Optimization

In warehouses with a high volume of inbound and outbound shipments, AI-driven predictive analytics can help optimize transportation routes, minimizing fuel costs, delivery times, and environmental impact.

Enhanced Delivery Efficiency: Predictive models analyze traffic patterns, weather conditions, and shipment volumes, recommending optimal delivery routes to improve delivery speed and reduce costs.

Lower Environmental Impact: By optimizing routes and minimizing unnecessary travel, predictive analytics supports sustainable practices in warehouses, reducing the carbon footprint associated with logistics.

3. Use of AI-Powered Cameras and Sensors for Quality Control and Anomaly Detection

AI-powered cameras and sensors play a critical role in quality control and anomaly detection, ensuring that warehouses maintain high standards in product quality and operational efficiency.

Quality Control

AI-driven cameras and sensors inspect products for defects or inconsistencies, catching quality issues early in the production or distribution process. Unlike traditional inspection methods, which are often manual and prone to error, AI-enabled systems are faster, more accurate, and capable of continuous operation.

Automated Defect Detection: AI-powered cameras use computer vision to detect defects, such as scratches, dents, or incorrect labeling, identifying quality issues with high precision. This allows warehouses to filter out defective items before they reach customers, reducing returns and maintaining brand reputation.

Consistency in Quality Standards: AI systems apply consistent criteria for quality inspections, ensuring uniform quality control across all products, batches, or locations, regardless of staff turnover or human error.

Anomaly Detection

AI-powered sensors and cameras continuously monitor warehouse conditions, identifying any unusual patterns or deviations from expected norms. Anomaly detection is essential for maintaining inventory integrity, facility safety, and equipment performance.

Real-Time Hazard Detection: AI-powered cameras monitor warehouse aisles and storage areas, identifying potential hazards, such as misplaced items, spills, or obstructions, alerting staff to take corrective action immediately.

Inventory Anomalies: AI systems analyze inventory patterns, flagging any irregularities, such as unexpected stock shortages or items in incorrect locations, which could indicate errors or theft.

Equipment Monitoring for Early Failure Detection: Sensors track equipment performance metrics, such as vibration, temperature, and speed. If these metrics exceed acceptable ranges, the AI system alerts maintenance teams to inspect the equipment, preventing unexpected breakdowns.

Case Study: Amazon's Use of AI for Quality and Anomaly Detection

Amazon has implemented AI-powered cameras and sensors in its warehouses to enhance quality control and ensure efficient operations. Amazon's system uses computer vision to inspect items for damage or labeling errors before shipment, ensuring only high-quality products reach customers. Additionally, AI systems monitor worker safety, detecting unsafe behaviors or potential hazards and alerting supervisors in real time. This proactive approach has allowed Amazon to maintain high quality standards while minimizing workplace accidents.

AI and data analytics have transformed warehouse management by enabling accurate demand forecasting, optimized inventory management, and streamlined workflows. Through predictive analytics, warehouses can make proactive decisions, ensuring that resources are efficiently allocated and potential issues are addressed before they impact operations. Furthermore, AI-powered cameras and sensors enhance quality control and anomaly detection, allowing warehouses to maintain high standards while improving safety and efficiency. As AI and data analytics continue to evolve, smart warehouses will become more autonomous, adaptive, and capable of meeting the complex demands of modern supply chains.

Digital Twins in Warehouse Operations

- ❖ 1. Explanation of digital twins and their role in warehouse management.

- ❖ 2. How digital twins enable virtual simulations, testing, and planning.

- ❖ 3. Real-world examples of digital twin applications in warehousing.

The concept of digital twins is transforming warehouse management by enabling virtual simulations, predictive analysis, and advanced planning capabilities. Digital twins are virtual replicas of physical assets, processes, or systems that mirror the real-world characteristics of warehouses, creating a bridge between the physical and digital spaces. This technology enables warehouse operators to model, test, and optimize operations in a virtual environment before implementing changes in real life, improving efficiency, reducing risk, and supporting proactive decision-making. In this section, we'll examine digital twins' role in warehouse operations, their functionality, and some real-world examples of their application.

1. Explanation of Digital Twins and Their Role in Warehouse Management

A digital twin is essentially a digital replica or virtual model of a physical entity—in this case, a warehouse, its layout, assets, and processes. This digital counterpart is constantly updated with real-time data from its physical counterpart through sensors, IoT devices, and other connected technologies. By integrating data from equipment, inventory, environmental conditions, and personnel movements, digital twins provide a comprehensive and dynamic view of warehouse operations.

The Key Components of a Digital Twin

Data Collection: Sensors and IoT devices gather real-time data from the warehouse, such as temperature, humidity, inventory levels, and equipment status.

Data Integration: This data is integrated with historical information and predictive models to create a comprehensive and continuously updated digital model.

Simulation and Analysis: The digital twin uses this data to run simulations, identify patterns, predict outcomes, and make recommendations.

Feedback Loop: The system allows warehouse managers to adjust operations virtually and observe the potential impact before implementing changes in the physical environment.

The Role of Digital Twins in Warehouse Operations

Digital twins support a wide range of applications in warehouse management:

Inventory and Space Optimization: By monitoring and simulating storage patterns and space utilization, digital twins help optimize layout and inventory placement to maximize storage efficiency and reduce retrieval times.

Predictive Maintenance: Digital twins can monitor the condition of equipment and predict when maintenance will be needed, minimizing unplanned downtime and extending the lifespan of assets.

Process Optimization: Digital twins allow for the testing and optimization of workflows, such as picking and packing, in a virtual environment to ensure maximum efficiency.

Safety and Compliance: Digital twins can analyze personnel movements, equipment usage, and environmental conditions to detect safety risks and support compliance with health and safety regulations.

2. How Digital Twins Enable Virtual Simulations, Testing, and Planning

One of the most powerful aspects of digital twins is their ability to conduct virtual simulations, test various scenarios, and support strategic planning in a risk-free digital environment. This functionality allows warehouse managers to evaluate potential improvements, predict the impact of changes, and identify optimal solutions without disrupting day-to-day operations.

Virtual Simulations

With digital twins, warehouse managers can simulate various scenarios, such as increased order volume, changes in picking routes, or the introduction of new automation technologies. By simulating these scenarios, digital twins provide valuable insights into potential bottlenecks, inefficiencies, and risks before they occur.

Example: During peak seasons, a digital twin can simulate an increased workload to identify potential congestion points in the picking and packing processes. This allows warehouse managers to adjust schedules or add temporary storage to accommodate the influx.

Testing and Troubleshooting

Digital twins also enable testing of new strategies or technologies, helping warehouse operators troubleshoot issues in a controlled virtual environment before applying changes in the physical warehouse. This reduces the risk of unforeseen disruptions and costly adjustments.

Example: A warehouse could test the impact of implementing robotic picking systems by simulating their integration within the digital twin. This would reveal potential layout adjustments, workflow impacts, and training requirements for employees.

Strategic Planning

Digital twins support long-term planning by enabling warehouse operators to evaluate the effects of strategic decisions, such as expanding the facility, integrating new technologies, or shifting inventory policies. This empowers managers to make data-driven decisions with confidence.

Example: A company planning to introduce a new product line can use a digital twin to simulate the additional storage and handling requirements, evaluating different layout adjustments to minimize disruption and optimize space utilization.

3. Real-World Examples of Digital Twin Applications in Warehousing

Several major companies have adopted digital twin technology to improve warehouse efficiency, enhance predictive capabilities, and support strategic planning. Here are some real-world examples that illustrate the versatility of digital twins in warehousing:

1. Siemens

Siemens, a leader in digital technology, has implemented digital twins in its own warehouses to enhance efficiency and streamline operations. By creating digital replicas of their facilities, Siemens can simulate different workflows, optimize resource allocation, and test automation technologies. The digital twins also provide real-time visibility into equipment performance, allowing Siemens to perform predictive maintenance and minimize downtime.

2. Amazon

Amazon uses digital twin technology to optimize warehouse layouts, streamline order-picking processes, and improve inventory management. By creating virtual replicas of its fulfillment centers, Amazon can model and test the impact of various layout configurations and automation strategies on throughput, accuracy, and efficiency. Amazon's digital twins also facilitate simulations for peak demand periods, helping the company to prepare for high-order volumes during events like Black Friday and Cyber Monday.

3. General Electric (GE)

GE has adopted digital twin technology in its distribution warehouses to monitor and manage inventory and assets. By implementing sensors and IoT devices across their facilities, GE's digital twins track real-time data on product location, environmental conditions, and equipment status. This enables GE to maintain optimal conditions for sensitive inventory items, manage stock levels effectively, and ensure timely maintenance for warehouse machinery.

4. Procter & Gamble (P&G)

Procter & Gamble utilizes digital twins to improve supply chain efficiency across its global distribution network. By simulating warehouse workflows, inventory movement, and storage capacity, P&G can optimize its logistics operations and improve order fulfillment times. Digital twins also help P&G test different warehouse management strategies and adjust processes to meet changing customer demands without compromising quality or service.

5. BMW

BMW employs digital twins in its automotive parts warehouses to streamline operations and improve accuracy in inventory management. By creating a digital replica of its warehouses, BMW can simulate workflows, optimize picking routes, and monitor environmental conditions for sensitive automotive components. Digital twins also enable BMW to manage its inventory more effectively, ensuring that parts are available when needed and reducing storage costs.

Digital twins represent a powerful tool for smart warehousing, providing real-time insights, enabling virtual simulations, and supporting strategic decision-making. By creating digital replicas of warehouse operations, digital twins allow businesses to anticipate challenges, test potential improvements, and optimize processes without disrupting daily operations. From predictive maintenance to inventory management and workflow optimization, digital twins offer unparalleled visibility and control over warehouse operations. Companies like Siemens, Amazon, and BMW have demonstrated the effectiveness of digital twins in achieving greater efficiency, reducing operational risks, and enhancing customer satisfaction. As digital twin technology continues to evolve, it will undoubtedly play an increasingly central role in the future of smart warehousing.

Smart Inventory Management and Demand Forecasting

- ❖ 1. Techniques for automating and optimizing inventory management.

- ❖ 2. How smart warehouses achieve near-perfect inventory accuracy.

- ❖ 3. AI-driven demand forecasting for just-in-time inventory. please write minimum 2000 words about it

In today's rapidly evolving business landscape, maintaining optimal inventory levels and accurately forecasting demand are crucial to effective warehouse management. Smart warehouses leverage cutting-edge technologies such as IoT, artificial intelligence (AI), and machine learning to streamline inventory management and improve demand forecasting. This chapter explores various techniques for automating and optimizing inventory management, achieving high levels of inventory accuracy, and utilizing AI-driven demand forecasting to enable just-in-time (JIT) inventory strategies.

1. Techniques for Automating and Optimizing Inventory Management

The traditional methods of managing inventory are time-consuming, labor-intensive, and often prone to human error. Smart warehouses, by contrast, employ automation and advanced technologies to significantly enhance inventory management processes, reduce errors, and optimize stock levels. Key techniques include:

a. Radio Frequency Identification (RFID) and Barcode Scanning

RFID and barcode scanning are fundamental to modern inventory management, providing quick and accurate tracking of products throughout the warehouse. RFID tags, which can be read from a distance without requiring a direct line of sight, allow for continuous tracking of items in real time. Barcode scanners, used at various points in the warehouse, also contribute to streamlined product tracking, ensuring that inventory data is consistently updated.

Benefits: Improved accuracy, faster processing times, and reduced manual data entry. RFID tags, in particular, are valuable for real-time visibility, which is essential in fast-moving warehouses.

b. Automated Storage and Retrieval Systems (AS/RS)

AS/RS includes various forms of automated equipment, such as shuttles, cranes, and robotic systems, that manage the placement and retrieval of inventory within the warehouse. These systems are particularly effective in large, high-density warehouses where manual retrieval would be inefficient.

Benefits: AS/RS improves storage density, increases picking speed, and reduces the need for manual labor, thus lowering operational costs and minimizing errors.

c. Drones for Inventory Counting

Drones are increasingly used in smart warehouses for periodic inventory counts and stock verification. Equipped with cameras and scanning technology, drones can navigate warehouse aisles autonomously, scanning inventory levels without interrupting normal warehouse operations. They provide a faster, more efficient alternative to manual stock counts, which are typically labor-intensive.

Benefits: Enhanced accuracy and efficiency in stock counting, reduced downtime for physical inventories, and minimized labor costs associated with cycle counting.

d. Autonomous Mobile Robots (AMRs)

AMRs are designed to navigate independently within the warehouse, transporting goods from one location to another.

These robots can assist in picking and replenishment activities, reducing the time and labor required for moving items across large facilities.

Benefits: Improved efficiency in picking and replenishment processes, reduced travel time within the warehouse, and minimized worker fatigue, which leads to a safer and more productive environment.

e. Predictive Maintenance for Equipment

In a smart warehouse, predictive maintenance technologies monitor the condition of equipment, such as forklifts and conveyor belts, to prevent breakdowns. By using IoT sensors and data analytics, warehouses can detect early signs of wear and tear, scheduling maintenance activities before issues arise.

Benefits: Reduced downtime, extended equipment lifespan, and minimized costs associated with unexpected repairs.

2. How Smart Warehouses Achieve Near-Perfect Inventory Accuracy

Inventory accuracy is essential for fulfilling orders efficiently, maintaining customer satisfaction, and reducing costs associated with overstocking or stockouts. In smart warehouses, the integration of advanced technologies facilitates near-perfect inventory accuracy through real-time tracking, intelligent data management, and automation.

a. Real-Time Data Synchronization

One of the main advantages of smart warehouses is the continuous synchronization of inventory data. Technologies like IoT, RFID, and barcoding allow for real-time tracking of inventory movement, ensuring that stock levels are updated instantly. This capability is critical for multi-channel operations, where multiple sales channels need to access accurate stock information simultaneously.

Benefits: Real-time synchronization reduces discrepancies in inventory records, enabling more accurate stock levels, efficient replenishment, and reduced risk of stockouts or overstocking.

b. Perpetual Inventory System

A perpetual inventory system continuously tracks inventory transactions through automated systems, allowing for real-time inventory accuracy. In this system, every time an item is received, picked, or moved within the warehouse, it is instantly recorded, creating a seamless and accurate record of stock levels.

Benefits: Near-perfect inventory accuracy, reduced need for physical inventory checks, and improved data visibility for decision-making.

c. Advanced Inventory Counting Techniques

Traditional physical inventories can be time-consuming and prone to error. Smart warehouses employ techniques like cycle counting, which involves counting small portions of inventory on a regular basis. Drones and robots equipped with cameras and scanning technology automate cycle counting, allowing for accurate stock verification without interrupting warehouse operations.

Benefits: Increased efficiency in stock counting, reduced reliance on full physical inventories, and enhanced inventory accuracy.

d. Machine Vision and AI-Powered Inspection

Machine vision, combined with AI, is used to detect discrepancies, such as misplaced or mislabeled items. Smart cameras installed on robots or at strategic locations in the warehouse can scan items, verify labels, and ensure that products are stored in the correct locations.

Benefits: Reduced errors in inventory placement, higher accuracy in stock levels, and improved picking accuracy, which enhances order fulfillment.

e. Cross-Functional Data Integration

Smart warehouses integrate data across functions, including inventory, sales, and procurement, to provide a holistic view of stock levels. This data integration enables a unified approach to inventory management, where all relevant teams have access to real-time data and can collaborate on decisions related to stock levels and replenishment.

Benefits: Improved coordination across functions, better inventory control, and proactive decision-making, which contributes to near-perfect inventory accuracy.

3. AI-Driven Demand Forecasting for Just-In-Time (JIT) Inventory

Demand forecasting plays a crucial role in effective inventory management, helping warehouses predict future demand and optimize stock levels. With advancements in AI and machine learning, smart warehouses can now employ sophisticated demand forecasting models that provide highly accurate predictions. These models support just-in-time (JIT) inventory, where stock is ordered and replenished based on actual demand, minimizing the need for large stockpiles.

a. AI Algorithms for Predicting Demand

AI-driven demand forecasting uses advanced algorithms, including machine learning, to analyze historical sales data, seasonal trends, and other influencing factors. By processing large datasets and identifying patterns, these algorithms generate accurate demand forecasts, enabling warehouses to anticipate inventory needs more effectively.

Benefits: Reduced risk of overstocking or understocking, improved ability to meet customer demand, and minimized holding costs.

b. Machine Learning for Dynamic Inventory Management

Machine learning algorithms continuously learn from new data, allowing warehouses to dynamically adjust inventory levels based on changes in demand. For instance, if demand for a particular product suddenly spikes, the system can recognize this trend and adjust stock levels accordingly. This dynamic approach to inventory management ensures that warehouses can respond quickly to market fluctuations.

Benefits: Increased responsiveness to demand changes, reduced stockouts, and minimized wastage from excess inventory.

c. Predictive Analytics for Seasonal and Event-Driven Demand

Seasonal trends, holidays, and events can have a significant impact on demand. Predictive analytics, powered by AI, can identify these trends and adjust inventory accordingly. For example, a warehouse may stock up on specific items in anticipation of a holiday season based on historical data and current market conditions.

Benefits: Improved preparation for seasonal demand spikes, minimized last-minute stock adjustments, and enhanced customer satisfaction through reliable stock availability.

d. JIT Inventory and Demand Forecasting Synergy

AI-driven demand forecasting enables just-in-time (JIT) inventory management by providing precise predictions about when stock is needed. By aligning inventory levels with actual demand, warehouses can reduce storage costs and minimize inventory waste. JIT inventory is especially valuable in industries where products have a limited shelf life or where holding costs are high.

Benefits: Lowered inventory holding costs, reduced risk of stock obsolescence, and improved cash flow due to minimized excess stock.

e. Real-World Examples of AI-Driven Demand Forecasting

Amazon: Amazon leverages AI-driven demand forecasting to manage its vast inventory and ensure that products are available to customers on time. By analyzing historical data, market trends, and customer behavior, Amazon optimizes its stock levels and enhances customer satisfaction.

Walmart: Walmart employs AI-powered demand forecasting models to accurately predict customer demand across its retail stores. This enables Walmart to maintain optimal stock levels, minimize stockouts, and reduce the costs associated with excess inventory.

Procter & Gamble (P&G): P&G utilizes AI-based demand forecasting to manage its global supply chain efficiently. The company's forecasting models analyze market trends and consumer behavior, allowing P&G to produce and stock products according to anticipated demand, thus reducing waste and optimizing production.

Smart inventory management and demand forecasting are critical components of an efficient smart warehouse. Through the integration of advanced technologies such as RFID, drones, AMRs, AI, and machine learning, warehouses achieve higher inventory accuracy, reduce operational costs, and optimize stock levels. Furthermore, AI-driven demand forecasting supports just-in-time inventory management, allowing warehouses to align stock levels with real demand, minimizing waste, and improving cash flow. As smart warehousing continues to evolve, these technologies will play an increasingly pivotal role in enabling companies to meet customer expectations, optimize resources, and maintain a competitive edge.

Energy-Efficient and Sustainable Smart Warehousing

- 1. Eco-friendly smart warehouse technologies: energy-efficient lighting, climate control, and renewable energy.

- 2. Benefits of sustainability in warehouses (cost-saving, eco-friendliness).

- 3. Case studies on warehouses implementing green initiatives.

As environmental concerns and sustainability initiatives continue to gain traction globally, the need for eco-friendly, energy-efficient warehousing solutions has become more pressing. Smart warehousing is not only about enhancing productivity and automation but also about minimizing environmental impact and optimizing resource use. This chapter examines the key eco-friendly technologies in smart warehouses, the benefits of sustainability, and case studies highlighting companies that have implemented green practices successfully.

1. Eco-Friendly Smart Warehouse Technologies: Energy-Efficient Lighting, Climate Control, and Renewable Energy

Incorporating energy-efficient technology and sustainable practices within warehouses reduces operational costs and aligns with corporate social responsibility (CSR) goals. Here's an in-depth look at the primary eco-friendly technologies used in modern smart warehouses:

a. Energy-Efficient Lighting Solutions

Lighting is one of the most significant energy consumers in warehousing, with large facilities requiring consistent illumination for safe and efficient operations. Transitioning to energy-efficient lighting, such as LED lights and smart lighting systems, can drastically reduce energy consumption.

LED Lighting: Compared to traditional incandescent or fluorescent lights, LED lights use up to 80% less energy and have a longer lifespan. They are also brighter, ensuring better visibility with reduced power use.

Motion-Activated Lighting: Smart warehouses often incorporate motion sensors in lighting systems, ensuring that lights are only activated when an area is in use. This practice minimizes unnecessary energy consumption and helps lower utility bills.

Daylight Harvesting: By using sensors to detect ambient sunlight, daylight harvesting systems automatically adjust indoor lighting levels. This approach is particularly useful in facilities with skylights or large windows, as it maximizes natural light while conserving electricity.

b. Climate Control and Smart HVAC Systems

In large warehouses, heating, ventilation, and air conditioning (HVAC) systems are essential for maintaining optimal working conditions and protecting temperature-sensitive goods. Smart HVAC systems optimize climate control based on real-time data, improving energy efficiency and lowering costs.

Smart Thermostats and Sensors: These devices regulate temperatures based on occupancy and external weather conditions. For instance, smart thermostats lower energy use during low-traffic periods by reducing heating or cooling levels in unoccupied zones.

Zone-Based Climate Control: By dividing the warehouse into different zones, zone-based climate control tailors temperatures to each area's needs. This approach is particularly useful for warehouses with mixed storage requirements (e.g., cold storage and ambient areas) as it conserves energy by avoiding overcooling or overheating.

Ventilation and Insulation: Efficient insulation minimizes the exchange of heat between indoor and outdoor environments, reducing the workload on HVAC systems. Additionally, well-designed ventilation systems improve air quality and maintain a stable climate, which helps in reducing energy usage.

c. Renewable Energy Sources

Utilizing renewable energy sources like solar and wind power is becoming increasingly popular among sustainable smart warehouses. These energy sources not only reduce dependence on fossil fuels but also provide a long-term solution for lowering operational costs and reducing carbon footprints.

Solar Panels: Solar panels installed on warehouse rooftops generate electricity to power lighting, HVAC systems, and other equipment. This not only lowers reliance on the grid but also contributes to overall energy cost savings.

Wind Turbines: Some warehouses located in windy regions incorporate small-scale wind turbines to generate electricity. While not as common as solar panels, wind power can be a valuable addition for warehouses seeking energy diversification.

Battery Storage: Renewable energy sources can be unpredictable, so some warehouses use battery storage systems to store excess energy generated by solar panels or wind turbines. This stored energy can be used during peak hours or as a backup, enhancing energy security and grid independence.

2. Benefits of Sustainability in Warehouses

Integrating sustainability into warehouse operations brings both environmental and economic advantages. Here are the primary benefits of implementing sustainable practices in warehouses:

a. Cost Savings

Energy-efficient technologies, such as LED lighting, smart HVAC systems, and renewable energy sources, reduce electricity and fuel costs. Although some eco-friendly upgrades require an upfront investment, they often result in substantial long-term savings. For instance, LED lights last longer and consume less power, which reduces both replacement and electricity costs over time.

Example: A warehouse that installs solar panels may benefit from lower electricity bills, as the facility can draw power from solar energy during peak daylight hours, reducing grid dependency.

b. Enhanced Brand Image and Corporate Responsibility

As environmental consciousness grows among consumers, companies with a strong commitment to sustainability gain a competitive edge. Sustainable warehousing demonstrates a company's dedication to environmental stewardship, enhancing its brand reputation and appeal to eco-conscious customers.

CSR Compliance: Sustainable practices are often part of corporate social responsibility (CSR) requirements. Green initiatives demonstrate compliance with CSR goals and help companies meet regulatory standards, improving relations with stakeholders, partners, and regulators.

c. Improved Employee Health and Safety

Eco-friendly warehouses with energy-efficient lighting, ventilation, and temperature control provide a safer and more comfortable work environment. Adequate lighting and temperature regulation reduce the risk of accidents and health issues, contributing to better employee productivity and satisfaction.

d. Reduced Environmental Impact

Sustainable warehouses minimize their environmental footprint by reducing greenhouse gas emissions, conserving natural resources, and using renewable energy. These practices contribute to broader environmental goals, such as combating climate change and preserving ecosystems.

Example: A smart warehouse powered by solar and wind energy significantly reduces its carbon footprint, contributing to the fight against global warming and reducing reliance on non-renewable energy.

e. Operational Efficiency and Long-Term Viability

Sustainable practices, such as waste reduction and efficient energy use, streamline warehouse operations and contribute to long-term operational efficiency. As energy prices fluctuate, reliance on renewable energy sources and efficient technology offers stability and resilience, ensuring the warehouse remains cost-effective in the face of market changes.

3. Case Studies on Warehouses Implementing Green Initiatives

Numerous companies have made strides in integrating sustainable practices into their warehouse operations. Below are examples of organizations that have successfully implemented eco-friendly solutions in their warehouses:

a. Amazon's Net Zero Carbon Pledge

Amazon has pledged to achieve net-zero carbon emissions by 2040. As part of this commitment, the company has incorporated several green initiatives in its warehouses, including solar panels on facility rooftops, LED lighting systems, and electric delivery vehicles. Amazon's efforts have significantly reduced its overall carbon footprint, and the company continues to invest in renewable energy projects globally to power its operations.

Key Initiatives: Solar panels on warehouse rooftops, electric vehicles, energy-efficient lighting, and water conservation practices.

b. Walmart's Renewable Energy Strategy

Walmart has set an ambitious goal to be powered 100% by renewable energy. The company has invested in solar panels, energy-efficient lighting, and refrigeration systems in its distribution centers. Walmart also focuses on waste reduction, using eco-friendly packaging materials and recycling initiatives to minimize its environmental impact.

Key Initiatives: Renewable energy (solar and wind), LED lighting, energy-efficient refrigeration, and waste management practices.

c. IKEA's Commitment to Sustainable Warehousing

IKEA has long been recognized for its commitment to sustainability. Its warehouses and distribution centers utilize renewable energy sources, including solar and wind power, and the company aims to achieve 100% renewable energy use in its operations. IKEA also uses energy-efficient lighting and advanced HVAC systems to optimize energy consumption in its facilities.

Key Initiatives: Renewable energy, energy-efficient lighting and HVAC, eco-friendly building materials, and waste reduction.

d. Prologis Green Warehouses

Prologis, a global leader in logistics real estate, has pioneered the concept of green warehouses by integrating energy-efficient technologies and sustainable practices. Prologis facilities use LED lighting, advanced HVAC systems, and solar panels, and the company focuses on sustainable building designs, such as green roofs and high-efficiency insulation.

Key Initiatives: Solar energy, LED lighting, energy-efficient building materials, and water conservation.

The shift towards energy-efficient and sustainable smart warehousing aligns with the growing focus on environmental responsibility and cost-efficiency. By incorporating technologies such as LED lighting, climate-controlled systems, and renewable energy sources, companies can create eco-friendly warehouses that reduce operational costs and minimize environmental impact. The case studies of Amazon, Walmart, IKEA, and Prologis demonstrate that sustainable warehousing is not only feasible but also highly beneficial for both businesses and the planet. As these technologies continue to evolve, smart warehouses will play a crucial role in advancing sustainability, ultimately creating greener and more resilient supply chains for the future.

Cybersecurity in Smart Warehousing

- *1. Importance of cybersecurity in connected warehouses.*
- *2. Threats to smart warehouse systems and best practices for securing them.*
- *3. Building a resilient smart warehouse infrastructure.*

As warehouses integrate advanced technologies, from IoT devices and AI-driven systems to robotics and cloud-based Warehouse Management Systems (WMS), they become increasingly vulnerable to cyber threats. Smart warehouses rely on interconnected systems to maintain efficiency and accuracy, but this connectivity also introduces risks to data integrity, operational continuity, and asset security. Cybersecurity, therefore, is crucial for protecting sensitive data, preserving operational efficiency, and safeguarding customer trust. This chapter examines the importance of cybersecurity in smart warehouses, the threats they face, best practices for protecting them, and how to build a resilient smart warehouse infrastructure.

1. Importance of Cybersecurity in Connected Warehouses

In the digital era, where smart warehouses use real-time data and automation, cybersecurity is more important than ever. Without robust security protocols, even minor breaches can compromise sensitive information, cause significant operational disruptions, and impact business continuity. Here are some reasons why cybersecurity is essential in smart warehousing:

a. Protection of Sensitive Data

Smart warehouses manage vast amounts of sensitive data, from inventory records and supplier information to customer data and transaction histories. This data is often shared across platforms and stakeholders, making it susceptible to interception if not adequately secured. Cybersecurity measures are essential to protect this information from unauthorized access and ensure compliance with data protection regulations.

b. Continuity of Operations

Smart warehouses rely on IoT devices, automated machinery, and real-time analytics to function effectively. A cyberattack that targets these systems can disrupt operations, halt production, or cause delays in order fulfillment. Ensuring cybersecurity mitigates such risks, allowing the warehouse to maintain seamless and uninterrupted operations.

c. Mitigating Financial Losses

A cybersecurity incident can lead to significant financial losses from downtime, ransom payments, data recovery, and the need for remedial security upgrades. Breaches can also result in fines for non-compliance with data protection laws. Investing in cybersecurity helps prevent these costs by proactively securing systems against potential threats.

d. Preserving Brand Reputation and Customer Trust

Security breaches erode customer trust and can damage a brand's reputation. Customers expect their data to be handled securely, and a breach can lead to reputational damage that's challenging to repair. By implementing stringent cybersecurity measures, warehouses demonstrate a commitment to safeguarding customer information, which builds confidence and enhances brand loyalty.

2. Threats to Smart Warehouse Systems

Understanding the potential threats to smart warehouses is the first step toward building a secure infrastructure. Cyber threats in smart warehousing come in various forms, and each can target different aspects of warehouse operations. Here are the primary threats that warehouses face:

a. Data Breaches and Unauthorized Access

Hackers often target warehouse systems to steal sensitive information, such as supplier contracts, customer data, and inventory records. Unauthorized access can occur through weak passwords, unpatched software vulnerabilities, or unsecured network devices. Once attackers gain access, they can extract data or alter records, leading to potential financial and operational repercussions.

b. Ransomware and Malware Attacks

Ransomware attacks have become increasingly common in warehouses and logistics. Attackers infiltrate a system, encrypt files, and demand a ransom to restore access. Malware, on the other hand, can infiltrate networks through malicious emails, compromised websites, or infected USB devices, damaging systems, and corrupting data.

c. IoT Vulnerabilities

Smart warehouses use IoT devices for inventory tracking, environmental monitoring, and asset management. However, these devices can be vulnerable to cyberattacks if they lack proper security protocols. IoT devices often have limited processing power, making it difficult to implement complex security measures, which can leave them open to attack.

d. Insider Threats

Not all threats come from outside the organization; sometimes, employees or contractors pose risks to warehouse security. Insider threats include unintentional actions, such as mishandling data, or deliberate acts, such as data theft. Implementing role-based access controls and monitoring user activity can help minimize these risks.

e. Distributed Denial of Service (DDoS) Attacks

DDoS attacks overwhelm a network with excessive traffic, rendering systems inaccessible. In a smart warehouse, a DDoS attack could disrupt the Warehouse Management System (WMS) or other critical applications, halting operations and causing delays.

3. Best Practices for Securing Smart Warehouses

Smart warehouses need comprehensive cybersecurity strategies that address both technological vulnerabilities and human factors. The following best practices can help protect warehouse systems and ensure robust cybersecurity:

a. Secure Access Controls

Implementing strong access controls is essential to prevent unauthorized users from accessing sensitive systems and data. This includes:

Role-Based Access Control (RBAC): Limit system access to authorized personnel only, assigning roles based on specific job responsibilities.

Multi-Factor Authentication (MFA): Add an extra layer of security to user accounts by requiring additional authentication steps, such as a one-time code sent to a mobile device.

Password Management: Enforce strong password policies and encourage the use of password managers to avoid common vulnerabilities.

b. Regular Software Updates and Patch Management

Outdated software is a common entry point for cyber attackers. Regularly updating warehouse management software, IoT firmware, and other applications helps close known security vulnerabilities. Automated patch management solutions can streamline the process, ensuring all systems are up-to-date with the latest security patches.

c. Network Segmentation

Separating different parts of the warehouse network (e.g., IoT devices, WMS, and administrative systems) limits the spread of potential attacks. In the event of a security breach in one segment, network segmentation prevents attackers from moving laterally across systems, protecting critical areas from unauthorized access.

d. Implement Firewalls and Intrusion Detection Systems (IDS)

Firewalls act as a barrier between trusted and untrusted networks, controlling incoming and outgoing traffic based on security policies. Additionally, Intrusion Detection Systems (IDS) monitor for unusual activity and alert administrators to potential threats. Together, firewalls and IDS help protect the warehouse from external attacks.

e. IoT Device Security

Securing IoT devices is critical in a smart warehouse. To protect these devices:

Use Secure Firmware: Ensure all IoT devices have secure firmware with built-in security features.

Device Authentication: Require IoT devices to authenticate themselves before connecting to the network.

Disable Unnecessary Functions: Reduce potential vulnerabilities by disabling unused features or ports on IoT devices.

f. Employee Training and Awareness

Human error is a leading cause of cybersecurity incidents. Regular training sessions educate employees on cybersecurity best practices, such as recognizing phishing emails, creating strong passwords, and handling sensitive data securely. Employees who are aware of potential threats are better equipped to avoid risky behavior.

g. Data Encryption

Data encryption ensures that sensitive information remains secure even if it's intercepted by unauthorized users.

Encrypting data at rest (stored data) and in transit (data being transmitted) protects it from unauthorized access.

4. Building a Resilient Smart Warehouse Infrastructure

Creating a resilient smart warehouse infrastructure involves combining cybersecurity measures with robust infrastructure planning to ensure security, reliability, and recovery. Here are some steps to achieve resilience:

a. Develop a Cybersecurity Framework

Establishing a cybersecurity framework tailored to the warehouse's needs helps define security policies, procedures, and response protocols. Frameworks like the National Institute of Standards and Technology (NIST) Cybersecurity Framework offer guidelines for identifying, protecting, detecting, responding to, and recovering from cyber threats.

b. Conduct Regular Security Audits and Vulnerability Assessments

Routine security audits identify potential weaknesses within the warehouse's infrastructure. Regular vulnerability assessments allow IT teams to proactively address issues before they are exploited by attackers.

c. Incident Response and Disaster Recovery Plans

An effective incident response plan outlines steps to follow in the event of a cybersecurity breach. This includes protocols for containing the attack, restoring operations, and communicating with stakeholders. Additionally, a disaster recovery plan details how to restore data and systems quickly to minimize downtime.

d. Invest in Cyber Insurance

Cyber insurance provides financial protection against cyber incidents, covering costs related to data breaches, ransomware attacks, and other cyber threats. For smart warehouses that rely heavily on interconnected systems, cyber insurance can be a valuable safety net in the event of a security incident.

Cybersecurity is an essential component of smart warehousing, as interconnected systems and digital data create both opportunities for efficiency and vulnerabilities to cyber threats. By implementing strong security practices, such as secure access controls, data encryption, IoT security, and employee training, warehouses can protect their assets, data, and operations from cyberattacks. Building a resilient infrastructure with incident response plans and cyber insurance further enhances a warehouse's ability to recover from potential security breaches. As smart warehousing continues to grow, maintaining robust cybersecurity will remain a priority for safeguarding assets, preserving customer trust, and ensuring operational continuity.

The Future of Smart Warehousing

❖ 1. Emerging technologies shaping the future: edge computing, blockchain, and 5G.

❖ 2. The potential impact of these technologies on warehouse operations.

❖ 3. Predictions and insights on the evolution of warehousing over the next decade.

The future of warehousing is inextricably linked to the ongoing advancements in technology. As industries continue to adopt automation, connectivity, and digital transformation, the evolution of smart warehouses is expected to accelerate rapidly. Emerging technologies like edge computing, blockchain, and 5G are poised to reshape how warehouses operate, improve efficiency, and enhance the overall supply chain ecosystem. This chapter explores these transformative technologies, their potential impact on warehouse operations, and offers predictions for the future of warehousing over the next decade.

1. Emerging Technologies Shaping the Future of Smart Warehousing: Edge Computing, Blockchain, and 5G

a. Edge Computing

Edge computing refers to the practice of processing data closer to where it is generated, rather than relying on a centralized cloud server. In smart warehouses, edge computing can drastically reduce latency and improve real-time data processing capabilities. With the sheer volume of data generated by IoT sensors, robotics, and automated systems in a warehouse, sending all this data to the cloud for processing can cause delays. By performing data processing at the edge, closer to the source (such as IoT devices or robots), edge computing allows for faster decision-making, reduced downtime, and improved responsiveness.

Application in Warehousing: In the context of smart warehousing, edge computing enables faster processing of inventory updates, condition monitoring of goods, and real-time tracking of assets. For instance, sensors embedded in warehouse racks or automated systems can instantly process inventory data on-site, sending only relevant insights or updates to the cloud, thus improving efficiency.

Impact on Operations: Edge computing enables faster decision-making, enhances automation, and supports the use of advanced AI-powered systems without lag. This technology is especially beneficial for time-sensitive operations, such as real-time stock management, predictive maintenance, and instant processing of inventory updates.

b. Blockchain

Blockchain is a decentralized, distributed ledger technology that ensures transparency, security, and immutability of transactions. In the context of smart warehousing, blockchain can provide an efficient and secure way to track goods through the entire supply chain, from the moment they are manufactured to their final destination in a warehouse.

Application in Warehousing: Blockchain can be used to create a secure and transparent inventory management system, where every transaction or movement of goods is recorded in an immutable ledger. This ensures that all parties involved in the supply chain — from suppliers to warehouses to customers — have access to accurate, real-time information about the location, condition, and status of goods.

Impact on Operations: By implementing blockchain, smart warehouses can significantly reduce the risk of fraud, errors, or discrepancies in inventory records. Blockchain also enhances traceability and accountability, improving both supply chain visibility and compliance with regulations. It facilitates seamless collaboration between different stakeholders by providing a transparent view of every transaction, thereby building trust across the supply chain.

c. 5G Connectivity

The rollout of 5G networks is set to revolutionize the connectivity infrastructure in warehouses. With significantly higher data transfer speeds, reduced latency, and the ability to support a greater number of connected devices simultaneously, 5G will address many of the connectivity challenges that current wireless technologies (like Wi-Fi) face in large-scale, high-density warehouse environments.

Application in Warehousing: 5G can support the continuous communication between various smart devices, from robots and drones to IoT sensors and wearable devices. This will improve the real-time monitoring and management of warehouse operations, enhancing automation and coordination across systems.

Impact on Operations: The increased bandwidth and speed of 5G will enable faster data transmission and communication between warehouse devices, enhancing the efficiency of automated systems. It will allow for smoother operation of remote-controlled equipment, autonomous robots, and drones, while also enabling more accurate and timely data collection. Additionally, 5G can enhance the effectiveness of augmented reality (AR) and virtual reality (VR) systems used in warehouse training and operations.

2. Potential Impact of These Technologies on Warehouse Operations

As edge computing, blockchain, and 5G continue to mature, their collective impact on warehouse operations will be profound, driving greater automation, efficiency, and connectivity. Here's how each of these technologies is expected to impact various aspects of warehouse operations:

a. Improved Efficiency and Automation

The integration of edge computing, blockchain, and 5G will significantly enhance automation within warehouses. Automation technologies, such as autonomous guided vehicles (AGVs), robotic arms, and drones, rely heavily on real-time data processing and high-speed communication. The ability to process data quickly at the edge, securely track goods with blockchain, and ensure continuous connectivity with 5G will lead to faster decision-making, smoother operations, and less downtime.

For example, autonomous vehicles in a warehouse could rely on edge computing to navigate the space, making real-time decisions about their movement based on sensor data. Simultaneously, blockchain could record every transaction related to the movement of goods, while 5G would ensure seamless communication across the entire system.

b. Enhanced Inventory Management

With the implementation of blockchain, warehouses will have access to a more secure and transparent system for tracking inventory throughout the supply chain. Smart contracts, powered by blockchain, could be used to automate processes such as stock replenishment, order fulfillment, and payments, ensuring that the right products are available at the right time.

Edge computing will also enhance inventory management by processing data from RFID tags, IoT sensors, and other smart devices located throughout the warehouse. This enables real-time inventory updates and minimizes stockouts or overstocking by improving demand forecasting.

c. Better Data Analytics and Predictive Maintenance

The use of real-time data, enabled by edge computing and 5G, will empower warehouses to better analyze and predict operational trends. Advanced data analytics platforms will be able to process large volumes of data generated by various sensors and IoT devices, providing valuable insights into warehouse performance, worker efficiency, and equipment usage.

With this data, warehouses can leverage predictive maintenance, identifying potential issues before they lead to equipment failure. This reduces downtime, improves asset longevity, and ensures smoother operations.

d. Increased Transparency and Security

Blockchain's ability to provide secure, transparent, and immutable records will ensure that warehouse operators, suppliers, and customers can trust the accuracy of data related to inventory movements. By utilizing blockchain, warehouses can streamline audits, improve compliance, and reduce the risk of fraud or errors in reporting.

3. Predictions and Insights on the Evolution of Warehousing Over the Next Decade

As these emerging technologies continue to evolve, the next decade will witness a complete transformation in warehouse operations. Here's a look at some key predictions for the future:

a. Highly Automated, Autonomous Warehouses

In the future, warehouses will increasingly rely on fully autonomous systems for their operations. AGVs, robots, drones, and AI-powered systems will handle everything from stock picking and sorting to packaging and shipping. This will lead to more streamlined and efficient operations, with reduced labor costs and minimal human intervention.

Edge computing and 5G will enable seamless communication between autonomous systems, ensuring that warehouses operate at peak efficiency, with real-time data constantly optimizing processes.

b. Data-Driven, AI-Powered Decision-Making

The future of warehousing will be data-driven, with AI and machine learning algorithms analyzing vast amounts of real-time data to optimize operations. Demand forecasting, inventory management, and even workforce scheduling will be powered by AI, enabling smarter decisions and greater flexibility in adapting to supply chain disruptions.

Blockchain will facilitate secure, transparent data sharing between parties, allowing AI systems to make more accurate predictions based on a complete view of the supply chain.

c. Hyper-Connected Supply Chains

The next decade will see an increasing number of warehouses integrated into highly interconnected supply chains. Blockchain, combined with IoT and 5G, will create a seamless flow of information across all stages of the supply chain. Real-time data will be shared securely between warehouses, suppliers, and retailers, enabling a more responsive and agile supply chain.

d. Sustainable and Green Warehouses

Sustainability will continue to be a key focus in warehouse design and operations. Energy-efficient technologies, powered by smart sensors and IoT, will help warehouses optimize their energy consumption. Blockchain and AI can also enable more sustainable supply chain practices by tracking and verifying the environmental impact of products.

The future of smart warehousing is bright, driven by the integration of cutting-edge technologies like edge computing, blockchain, and 5G. These innovations will enable warehouses to operate with greater efficiency, automation, and security, while also offering unprecedented levels of transparency and data-driven decision-making. As these technologies mature, warehouses will become more autonomous, agile, and connected, creating a more responsive and resilient supply chain. The next decade promises to revolutionize warehousing, and businesses that adopt these emerging technologies early will be well-positioned to lead the way in an increasingly competitive global market.

Case Studies and Real-World Applications

❖ *1.In-depth case studies of successful smart warehouses across different industries.*

❖ *2.Lessons learned from early adopters of smart warehouse technology.*

❖ *3.Key takeaways for businesses considering the transition to a smart warehouse.*

The concept of smart warehouses is no longer just theoretical—many organizations across industries are already embracing these advanced technologies to streamline operations, reduce costs, and increase productivity. This section delves into in-depth case studies of successful smart warehouses, providing insights into how these technologies are transforming operations in real-world settings. It also explores lessons learned from early adopters and highlights key takeaways for businesses considering transitioning to a smart warehouse.

1. In-Depth Case Studies of Successful Smart Warehouses Across Different Industries

a. Amazon – E-commerce Industry

Amazon, the global leader in e-commerce, is widely recognized for its advanced use of warehouse automation. Amazon's fulfillment centers leverage cutting-edge technologies such as robotics, AI, and machine learning to process millions of orders daily.

Technologies Used: Amazon has implemented autonomous mobile robots (AMRs) that transport shelves of products to human workers for picking. The robots are integrated with a sophisticated Warehouse Management System (WMS) that manages inventory and tracks product movements. The company also uses AI-powered algorithms to predict demand, optimize storage, and improve routing within warehouses.

Outcome: These innovations have drastically improved efficiency in Amazon's warehouses. The robots work alongside human employees, reducing the time it takes to fulfill orders and enhancing accuracy. In addition to robotics, AI and machine learning have been used to optimize inventory management and predict future demand, enabling Amazon to meet customer expectations for fast delivery times.

Key Takeaways: The use of robotics combined with AI and machine learning allows Amazon to maintain high operational efficiency, even as demand fluctuates. Their success highlights the importance of seamlessly integrating automation with human labor, as well as the potential of predictive analytics to optimize warehouse performance.

b. Zara — Retail Industry

Zara, the Spanish fashion retailer, has made significant strides in implementing smart warehouse technology as part of its strategy to enhance supply chain operations and inventory management.

Technologies Used: Zara's warehouses use RFID tags for real-time tracking of inventory. This technology is paired with a sophisticated data analytics platform that helps Zara monitor the movement of goods across its network of stores and warehouses. Zara has also adopted automated sorting systems and robotics to streamline the picking and packing process.

Outcome: RFID technology has allowed Zara to achieve greater inventory accuracy, reducing stockouts and ensuring that popular items are always available in stores. The automated sorting systems speed up the order fulfillment process, enabling Zara to respond quickly to changing fashion trends.

Key Takeaways: Zara's success with smart warehousing demonstrates the importance of integrating real-time inventory tracking into supply chain operations. RFID technology, combined with automation, not only improves efficiency but also enhances customer satisfaction by ensuring products are available when needed.

c. DHL – Logistics and Supply Chain Industry

DHL, a leading global logistics provider, has invested heavily in smart warehouse technology to improve its operations and service delivery. One of their notable initiatives is the development of fully automated warehouses in several countries.

Technologies Used: DHL has incorporated robotics, drones, and AI-powered systems to automate its warehouses. They use robots to handle material storage and retrieval tasks, while drones are employed for scanning and monitoring the warehouse environment. Additionally, DHL has developed an AI-driven system that assists in optimizing warehouse workflows and routing of products.

Outcome: DHL's smart warehouse initiatives have led to significant improvements in operational efficiency and cost reduction. The company has been able to increase the speed of order fulfillment, reduce human error, and provide real-time insights into inventory levels and product movements.

Key Takeaways: DHL's implementation of robotics and AI in warehouse operations illustrates the effectiveness of automating repetitive tasks and enhancing real-time decision-making. The use of drones for scanning and monitoring also shows how emerging technologies can be leveraged to improve safety and efficiency.

d. Walmart – Retail Industry

Walmart, the world's largest retailer, is pioneering the use of smart warehousing to support its global supply chain operations. The company is integrating various technologies to create a highly automated and efficient warehouse environment.

Technologies Used: Walmart's warehouses use automated guided vehicles (AGVs), robotics, and AI to manage the movement of goods within the facility. The company has also deployed machine learning algorithms to optimize inventory levels and demand forecasting. Additionally, Walmart is testing autonomous robots for cleaning and monitoring inventory in its warehouses.

Outcome: Walmart has achieved significant improvements in warehouse productivity by using AGVs and robotics to handle the movement of goods, reducing the need for manual labor and improving efficiency. The integration of machine learning for demand forecasting has helped Walmart to reduce inventory holding costs and optimize stock levels.

Key Takeaways: Walmart's smart warehouse technology highlights the importance of automation in reducing operational costs and increasing warehouse throughput. The company's use of machine learning to optimize inventory management underscores the growing role of data analytics in enhancing supply chain performance.

2. Lessons Learned from Early Adopters of Smart Warehouse Technology

a. The Importance of Integration

One of the key lessons learned from early adopters of smart warehouse technology is the importance of integrating various systems and technologies. A successful smart warehouse requires seamless communication between robotics, WMS, AI algorithms, IoT devices, and other automation tools. Disjointed or incompatible systems can lead to inefficiencies and downtime, which negates the benefits of automation.

Lesson: Businesses considering smart warehouse technology should prioritize system integration. This involves ensuring that all technologies are compatible and can communicate effectively with each other to optimize warehouse operations.

b. Data-Driven Decision Making

Another crucial lesson is the value of data-driven decision-making. Companies that have successfully implemented smart warehouses have relied heavily on data analytics and AI to optimize operations. Real-time data from IoT sensors, RFID tags, and other smart devices enable managers to make informed decisions that improve inventory accuracy, order fulfillment speed, and overall warehouse efficiency.

Lesson: Leveraging data analytics is essential for optimizing warehouse operations. Companies should invest in robust data collection and analysis systems to ensure that they can make real-time decisions based on accurate and up-to-date information.

c. Workforce Training and Adaptability

While automation can drastically improve efficiency, it is also critical to invest in workforce training. The shift to a smart warehouse often requires workers to adapt to new technologies, systems, and workflows. Without proper training and change management strategies, employees may struggle to adapt to new systems, which can lead to inefficiencies or resistance to automation.

Lesson: Companies should invest in ongoing training programs for their workforce to ensure smooth transitions to smart warehouse environments. Workforce adaptability is key to the successful implementation of new technologies.

d. Scalability and Flexibility

Scalability and flexibility are essential factors for long-term success. As demand fluctuates, warehouses need systems that can easily scale up or down to accommodate changes in order volumes. The ability to quickly adapt to new technologies or processes as they emerge is also critical in maintaining a competitive edge.

Lesson: Businesses should select smart warehouse solutions that are scalable and flexible to ensure they can evolve with changing market demands and technological advancements.

3. Key Takeaways for Businesses Considering the Transition to a Smart Warehouse

As more businesses consider transitioning to smart warehouse solutions, the following key takeaways will help ensure a successful implementation:

a. Start Small, Scale Gradually

Many businesses that have successfully implemented smart warehousing have done so in phases. Rather than overhauling the entire warehouse system at once, companies should begin with small pilot projects to test new technologies and workflows. Once the pilot is successful, the solution can be gradually scaled across the warehouse or to other locations.

b. Focus on ROI

While the initial investment in smart warehouse technology can be significant, the long-term benefits often outweigh the costs. Companies should focus on the potential return on investment (ROI) that can be realized through improved efficiency, cost savings, and enhanced customer satisfaction. Tracking metrics like inventory accuracy, order fulfillment speed, and operational costs will help businesses assess the success of their smart warehouse investments.

c. Adopt a Customer-Centric Approach

The ultimate goal of any smart warehouse initiative is to improve customer satisfaction. Businesses should ensure that their smart warehousing solutions are designed to meet customer expectations, particularly in terms of fast, accurate order fulfillment. Real-time inventory tracking, faster processing times, and the ability to offer personalized customer experiences are key benefits that businesses should focus on.

d. Invest in Future-Proof Technologies

The warehouse of the future will rely on emerging technologies like AI, machine learning, blockchain, and IoT. As such, businesses should prioritize investing in technologies that are adaptable and future-proof. This will ensure that their smart warehouse solutions remain relevant and competitive as technology continues to evolve.

The case studies of Amazon, Zara, DHL, and Walmart illustrate the transformative potential of smart warehouse technology across different industries. These companies have embraced automation, robotics, data analytics, and IoT to streamline operations, improve efficiency, and enhance customer satisfaction. However, as early adopters have learned, success in smart warehousing depends on effective integration, workforce training, and data-driven decision-making. Businesses considering the transition to a smart warehouse should focus on scalability, ROI, and adopting future-proof technologies to stay competitive in an increasingly digital supply chain environment.

Implementing a Smart Warehouse: Step-by-Step Guide

- ❖ *1.Key considerations before transitioning to a smart warehouse.*

- ❖ *2.Step-by-step approach to upgrading technology, training staff, and phasing in changes.*

- ❖ *3.Budgeting, planning, and ROI analysis for smart warehouse implementation.*

Transitioning to a smart warehouse involves a comprehensive approach that includes upgrading technology, training staff, and carefully planning the budgeting and ROI analysis. It requires careful thought, time, and commitment, but the benefits—improved operational efficiency, enhanced accuracy, cost savings, and a competitive edge—are substantial. Below is a step-by-step guide to implementing a smart warehouse.

1. Key Considerations Before Transitioning to a Smart Warehouse

Before embarking on the transition to a smart warehouse, it's essential to consider the following factors:

a. Business Objectives and Goals

Clearly define the reasons for transitioning to a smart warehouse. Is the goal to improve inventory accuracy, reduce lead times, improve customer satisfaction, or optimize space utilization? Understanding your business objectives will guide decisions about technology adoption and workflow changes. Be specific in how a smart warehouse will benefit your overall business goals.

b. Current Warehouse Capabilities

Evaluate the existing infrastructure, processes, and systems in your warehouse. Take stock of your current Warehouse Management System (WMS), inventory control methods, layout, and staffing. Identify the areas of improvement and inefficiencies that need to be addressed through automation, robotics, or other smart technologies.

c. Technology Compatibility

Consider the compatibility of existing systems with the new technologies you plan to implement. If your current WMS and ERP systems are outdated, you might need to upgrade them to integrate seamlessly with the new technologies, such as IoT sensors, AI, and robotics.

d. Scalability and Flexibility

The technology and solutions you adopt should be scalable, allowing for future expansion. Choose systems that can grow with your business and adapt to emerging technologies. Flexibility in the system is key, as new technologies or market changes may arise.

e. Workforce Readiness

Assess your workforce's readiness for the transition. Are your employees familiar with automation, robotics, and data-driven decision-making? How comfortable are they with adopting new technologies? It is crucial to plan for adequate training and possible resistance to change.

f. Budget and Resources

Transitioning to a smart warehouse requires significant investment. Ensure that you have the necessary resources to implement these technologies, and plan for the long-term return on investment (ROI). Factor in the costs for new technologies, training, and any potential disruptions during the implementation phase.

g. Security and Data Privacy

With smart warehouses relying heavily on data, IoT devices, and interconnected systems, cybersecurity is paramount. Ensure that the chosen technologies are secure and compliant with data privacy regulations. Identify any potential security risks in your systems and take appropriate measures to mitigate them.

2. Step-by-Step Approach to Upgrading Technology, Training Staff, and Phasing in Changes

a. Step 1: Assess and Design the Smart Warehouse Plan

Objective: This step focuses on understanding the current state and designing a roadmap for the transition to a smart warehouse.

Actions:

Perform a thorough analysis of existing systems, processes, and inefficiencies.

Define your goals and KPIs (e.g., reducing order fulfillment time, improving inventory accuracy).

Identify the technologies required (e.g., IoT, robotics, AI) and how they will interact within the warehouse.

Design an updated warehouse layout that accommodates automation, including dedicated spaces for robotics, drones, and inventory storage systems.

b. Step 2: Select the Right Technology and Vendor Partnerships

Objective: Choose the right technologies and systems that align with your business objectives.

Actions:

Select a Warehouse Management System (WMS) that integrates with new technologies (e.g., robotics, IoT, AI).

Consider adopting automation technologies such as Automated Guided Vehicles (AGVs), robotic arms, or drones for specific tasks like picking and packing.

Choose IoT solutions for real-time inventory tracking, environmental monitoring, and asset management.

Engage with vendors and partners who have experience implementing smart warehouse solutions in your industry.

c. Step 3: Plan for Data Integration and Infrastructure

Objective: Ensure seamless data flow between systems and devices.

Actions:

Integrate all technologies (WMS, ERP, robotics, IoT sensors) into one unified system.

Plan for the necessary IT infrastructure to support large amounts of real-time data processing and storage (e.g., cloud solutions, edge computing).

Implement sensors and devices to monitor warehouse conditions such as temperature, humidity, and inventory movements.

Set up a robust data analytics platform to analyze the data collected and optimize warehouse operations.

d. Step 4: Employee Training and Change Management

Objective: Ensure the workforce is prepared to adopt new technologies and workflows.

Actions:

Design training programs for employees to learn about new systems, including how to operate robotic systems and interact with automated technologies.

Train staff on the use of the new WMS and any other software platforms being introduced.

Implement a change management plan to address resistance to change and ensure smooth adaptation. This can include regular communication, involvement of key employees in the planning process, and phased rollouts of new systems.

e. Step 5: Pilot Testing and Phased Rollout

Objective: Test the new systems and technologies on a smaller scale before full implementation.

Actions:

Start with a pilot project in one section of the warehouse (e.g., picking and packing area). Deploy the new technologies, monitor performance, and make adjustments based on feedback.

Evaluate the results of the pilot project using key performance indicators (KPIs) such as order accuracy, speed of picking, and labor productivity.

Based on the success of the pilot, roll out the technology across the entire warehouse or multiple locations, making adjustments as needed.

f. Step 6: Ongoing Monitoring and Optimization

Objective: Continuously monitor warehouse performance and optimize systems to improve efficiency.

Actions:

Use real-time data from IoT sensors and other smart technologies to continuously monitor warehouse performance.

Regularly review KPIs and adjust processes to meet operational goals.

Implement a feedback loop from employees and system users to identify areas for further improvement.

Stay updated on new technologies and trends in the smart warehouse industry to keep your warehouse competitive and adaptable.

3. Budgeting, Planning, and ROI Analysis for Smart Warehouse Implementation

a. Budgeting for Smart Warehouse Transition

Technology Costs: These include the costs of acquiring and implementing new technologies such as robotics, IoT devices, AI systems, and automated equipment. This can also involve upgrades to your Warehouse Management System (WMS) and other software.

Infrastructure Costs: If the existing warehouse infrastructure is inadequate to support new technologies, additional investments in physical space and IT infrastructure (e.g., servers, cloud storage) may be required.

Training Costs: Staff training is a crucial aspect of the transition. Allocate a portion of the budget for employee training programs to ensure they are equipped to handle new technologies.

Maintenance and Support Costs: As with any new system, regular maintenance and support are required to ensure the longevity of the systems and equipment. Include service contracts and support costs in the budgeting plan.

b. Planning for Smart Warehouse Implementation

Timeline: Establish a clear timeline for each phase of the implementation. This includes planning for the assessment phase, selection of technologies, training, pilot testing, and full-scale deployment. A typical timeline could span from six months to a year, depending on the size and complexity of the warehouse.

Risk Management: Identify potential risks such as system failures, technology integration issues, and employee resistance to change. Prepare mitigation strategies to address these challenges and ensure the project stays on track.

Contingency Planning: Set aside a contingency budget to account for unforeseen costs or challenges that may arise during the implementation process.

c. ROI Analysis

Cost Savings: Calculate the potential cost savings from automating manual tasks such as order picking, packing, and inventory management. The reduction in labor costs, coupled with improvements in efficiency, should contribute significantly to ROI.

Operational Efficiency Gains: Estimate the improvements in order fulfillment speed, inventory accuracy, and warehouse throughput. Faster processing times and reduced errors contribute directly to enhanced customer satisfaction and revenue.

Long-Term Value: Consider the long-term value that smart warehouse technologies bring, including scalability, the ability to handle fluctuating demand, and future-proofing the warehouse for emerging technologies.

Payback Period: Calculate the payback period—the time it will take for the warehouse to recover the initial investment through operational improvements and cost savings. This will help justify the investment and demonstrate the financial benefits.

Implementing a smart warehouse is a significant undertaking that requires careful planning, investment, and change management. By following a structured approach, businesses can successfully transition to a smart warehouse environment, enhance operational efficiency, and achieve significant cost savings. Understanding the key considerations, taking a step-by-step approach to technology adoption and workforce training, and performing detailed budgeting and ROI analysis will ensure that the transition is seamless and yields long-term benefits.

Challenges and Limitations in Smart Warehousing

❖ *1. Common challenges businesses face (cost, integration, training, maintenance).*

❖ *2. Limitations of current smart technologies and how companies are overcoming them.*

❖ *3. Addressing the human factor: workforce adaptation and training for new technologies.*

While smart warehousing offers significant benefits, such as improved operational efficiency, reduced labor costs, and enhanced customer service, businesses face several challenges and limitations when adopting these technologies. These challenges can impact the speed and success of implementation. Below, we explore the common challenges, the limitations of current technologies, and how companies are overcoming these issues, especially with respect to workforce adaptation and training.

1. Common Challenges Businesses Face in Smart Warehousing

a. Cost of Implementation

The initial cost of implementing smart warehousing technologies is one of the most significant challenges businesses face. Technologies such as automation systems, robotics, Internet of Things (IoT) sensors, AI, and Warehouse Management Systems (WMS) require significant investment. For many companies, especially small and medium-sized businesses, the capital outlay can be prohibitively high.

Solution: Businesses can consider phased implementation, starting with the most critical areas where automation will provide the greatest return on investment (ROI). This could involve automating inventory tracking, order picking, or material handling. Additionally, exploring financing options or leasing agreements for equipment can spread costs over time, reducing the immediate financial burden.

b. Integration with Legacy Systems

Integrating new technologies with existing systems can be complex and costly. Many warehouses still rely on older

Warehouse Management Systems (WMS) or other manual processes that may not be compatible with newer automation and IoT technologies. The integration of these systems often requires custom development, which can increase the time and cost of the transition.

Solution: To address integration challenges, companies can gradually migrate to new systems, ensuring compatibility with legacy systems during the transition period. Partnering with technology providers who specialize in integration can help ensure that new systems work seamlessly with existing infrastructure. Also, cloud-based WMS solutions may offer easier integration and scalability compared to traditional on-premise systems.

c. Workforce Training and Adaptation

The introduction of advanced technologies like robotics, AI, and automation may be met with resistance from employees who fear job displacement or find it difficult to adapt to new systems. Adequate training and support are necessary for workers to feel comfortable using the new technologies and workflows.

Solution: Investing in a robust employee training program is essential to overcoming resistance and facilitating smoother transitions. Training should not only focus on the technical aspects of new systems but also emphasize the positive impacts these technologies will have on employee productivity and job satisfaction. Employee engagement in the decision-making process can also help build acceptance and readiness for change.

d. Ongoing Maintenance and Support

After the initial implementation, warehouses must maintain and update their smart technologies to ensure they remain efficient and secure. This includes regular maintenance of robotics and automation systems, updating software, and ensuring all devices, such as IoT sensors, remain in good working condition. The challenge is finding the right balance between operational uptime and the need for maintenance.

Solution: To minimize downtime, warehouses can adopt predictive maintenance strategies using IoT sensors to detect early signs of wear and tear in equipment. Establishing service level agreements (SLAs) with technology providers for ongoing support and maintenance can ensure that issues are addressed promptly. Additionally, creating in-house expertise or training staff to manage and maintain critical systems can help reduce reliance on external vendors.

2. Limitations of Current Smart Technologies and How Companies Are Overcoming Them

While smart warehouse technologies have transformed the logistics and supply chain industries, there are still limitations in current systems that may affect their efficiency or applicability in certain warehouse settings.

a. Limited Flexibility in Automation Systems

Most current automation systems, such as Automated Guided Vehicles (AGVs) or robotic arms, are designed for specific tasks and may not be adaptable to changes in the warehouse environment. For example, a robotic picking system optimized for a particular type of product may struggle to handle new, more complex products.

Solution: To overcome this limitation, companies are investing in more flexible and adaptable systems. For instance, advanced robotics equipped with AI can be programmed to handle various types of goods, adjusting their processes to different product shapes, sizes, and weights. Additionally, modular and scalable automation solutions allow for adjustments and updates as business needs evolve.

b. Challenges in Real-Time Data Processing

While IoT sensors and AI-powered systems can collect vast amounts of data, processing this data in real-time remains a challenge for many companies. The sheer volume of data generated by smart devices can overwhelm existing data management systems, leading to delays in decision-making or missed opportunities for optimization.

Solution: To address these data processing challenges, companies are turning to edge computing, where data is processed closer to the source of generation (e.g., within the warehouse). This reduces latency and ensures quicker decision-making. Additionally, cloud computing platforms with advanced data analytics capabilities are increasingly being used to analyze and derive actionable insights from large datasets in real-time.

c. Dependency on Connectivity and Network Reliability

Smart warehouses rely on continuous connectivity between devices, systems, and employees. Any disruption in the network, such as connectivity loss or system downtime, can lead to delays, errors, or even halt warehouse operations completely. Many smart systems are heavily dependent on Wi-Fi or other wireless technologies, which can be unreliable in certain environments.

Solution: To mitigate connectivity issues, companies are investing in redundant network systems and backup power solutions. For instance, using 5G networks can offer high-speed connectivity with greater reliability, while mesh networks can ensure seamless communication between devices even in areas with weak signal strength. Additionally, some companies are developing offline capabilities for critical systems, enabling certain functions to continue even if the network is temporarily unavailable.

d. Security Risks with Increased Connectivity

The more connected a warehouse becomes, the more vulnerable it is to cyberattacks. With the integration of IoT, robotics, and cloud-based WMS, smart warehouses present a larger attack surface for potential cybercriminals. Data breaches, system hacking, and ransomware attacks are growing concerns as warehouses store sensitive operational data.

Solution: To address these security risks, businesses are investing in advanced cybersecurity measures, including encrypted communications, multi-factor authentication (MFA), and continuous monitoring of networks for suspicious activities. Regular cybersecurity audits and updates to security protocols also play a critical role in protecting systems from evolving threats.

3. Addressing the Human Factor: Workforce Adaptation and Training for New Technologies

One of the most significant challenges in the implementation of smart warehouses is the human factor—ensuring that the workforce is ready to work with the new technologies and systems. Proper training and management of human resources are crucial to overcoming this challenge.

a. Workforce Resistance to Change

Employees may be resistant to new technologies due to concerns about job loss or difficulty in learning new systems. This resistance can slow down the adoption process and create friction in the workplace.

Solution: Engaging employees early in the process is key. Involve them in discussions about the benefits of automation and how it will improve their work environment rather than replace them. Emphasize that the goal is to reduce manual tasks, not jobs, and that technology will help them focus on more complex and strategic tasks. Additionally, providing career development opportunities related to new technologies (e.g., AI, robotics) can create enthusiasm for change.

b. Training for New Technologies

The rapid pace of technological advancement means that employees must continuously learn how to operate and maintain new systems. Ensuring that employees are adequately trained in using robotics, AI, WMS, and other smart warehouse technologies is crucial for maximizing efficiency and minimizing errors.

Solution: Develop comprehensive training programs that cover both the technical and practical aspects of working with new technologies. Use hands-on training sessions, simulations, and e-learning platforms to ensure that employees feel confident in their ability to operate the new systems. In addition, ongoing education and access to resources such as user manuals, webinars, and support networks will help employees stay up to date with advancements.

c. Creating a Collaborative Work Environment

As automation takes over routine tasks, the role of employees will shift to more strategic and decision-making functions. However, this transition requires a new type of workforce—one that can collaborate effectively with advanced technologies and bring in human expertise to enhance machine-driven processes.

Solution: Foster a culture of collaboration between humans and machines by encouraging employees to act as "supervisors" of automated systems. By combining the strengths of humans (creativity, problem-solving, adaptability) with the capabilities of smart technologies (speed, accuracy, scalability), companies can create a work environment where employees feel valued and integral to the process.

While smart warehousing offers tremendous advantages, including increased efficiency, reduced labor costs, and improved customer satisfaction, there are significant challenges and limitations that businesses must navigate. These include the cost of implementation, system integration issues, workforce training, and the limitations of current technologies. By addressing these challenges thoughtfully—through phased implementation, effective employee training, and investment in flexible and secure technologies—businesses can overcome barriers and successfully transition to smart warehouses. Understanding the human factor and ensuring that employees are supported during this transition is also critical for the long-term success of the smart warehouse transformation.

Conclusion: Smart Warehousing as a Competitive Advantage

❖ 1. Recap of the benefits of smart warehousing.

❖ 2. How smart warehousing creates a competitive edge in logistics and supply chain management.

❖ 3. Encouraging the adoption of smart technology for future-ready warehouse management.

As the logistics and supply chain industries continue to evolve, businesses are seeking innovative solutions to stay ahead of the competition. Smart warehousing, driven by technologies like automation, IoT, AI, and robotics, is emerging as a critical strategy for businesses aiming to enhance operational efficiency, reduce costs, and improve customer satisfaction. The adoption of smart technology in warehouse management not only streamlines operations but also offers businesses a substantial competitive edge.

1. Recap of the Benefits of Smart Warehousing

Smart warehousing offers a host of advantages that can significantly transform the way warehouses operate:

Increased Efficiency: Automation and robotics streamline processes like order picking, sorting, and packing, reducing human error and increasing throughput. Systems like Automated Guided Vehicles (AGVs) and robotic arms can operate continuously, ensuring faster and more accurate fulfillment of orders.

Cost Reduction: The initial investment in smart warehouse technologies may seem high, but the long-term benefits far outweigh the costs. Automation reduces the reliance on manual labor, lowers operational costs, and improves space utilization. Energy-efficient technologies and optimized inventory management also contribute to cost savings.

Improved Inventory Accuracy: Smart technologies such as IoT sensors, RFID tags, and real-time tracking systems ensure that inventory levels are accurate and up-to-date, reducing the risk of stockouts, overstocking, or order fulfillment errors.

Enhanced Customer Satisfaction: With faster, more accurate order fulfillment, businesses can meet customer expectations for quicker delivery times. Real-time inventory visibility allows for better communication with customers and more reliable service.

Data-Driven Insights: Advanced analytics, powered by AI and machine learning, enable businesses to optimize inventory management, predict demand trends, and improve forecasting. This data-driven approach leads to better decision-making and operational efficiency.

2. How Smart Warehousing Creates a Competitive Edge in Logistics and Supply Chain Management

Smart warehousing is more than just a way to improve warehouse operations; it plays a pivotal role in shaping the entire supply chain and logistics strategy. Here's how smart warehousing provides a competitive edge:

Faster Response Times: With the real-time visibility that smart technologies provide, businesses can quickly adapt to changes in demand, inventory fluctuations, or disruptions in the supply chain. This agility gives businesses an advantage in fast-paced markets where response time is critical.

Scalability and Flexibility: As customer demands grow or fluctuate, smart warehouses can quickly scale operations to accommodate increased volume. Automated systems can handle higher workloads without compromising performance, while AI systems can adjust workflows based on data insights. This scalability allows companies to meet the demands of growing or seasonal business cycles without investing in significant infrastructure changes.

Enhanced Collaboration and Transparency: The integration of smart technologies fosters collaboration among different stakeholders in the supply chain. IoT-enabled devices, cloud-based systems, and real-time data sharing allow for greater transparency across the supply chain, facilitating better communication between warehouses, suppliers, and customers. This transparency improves trust and reduces bottlenecks caused by miscommunication or delays.

Sustainability and Green Logistics: In addition to improving operational efficiency, smart warehousing also supports sustainability initiatives. Technologies like energy-efficient lighting, climate control systems, and the use of renewable energy sources reduce the environmental impact of warehouse operations. This is particularly important as businesses increasingly focus on eco-friendly practices to meet consumer demand for sustainable solutions.

Better Risk Management: Predictive analytics and IoT technologies help warehouses foresee potential risks, such as equipment failure, supply chain disruptions, or inventory shortages. By addressing these risks proactively, businesses can mitigate costly disruptions and maintain smooth operations.

3. Encouraging the Adoption of Smart Technology for Future-Ready Warehouse Management

The future of warehousing lies in the adoption of smart technology. To remain competitive in the rapidly changing logistics landscape, businesses must embrace the digital transformation of their warehouse operations. Here are some strategies for encouraging the adoption of smart warehouse technologies:

Start with a Roadmap: Transitioning to a smart warehouse doesn't need to be overwhelming. Businesses should create a clear roadmap that outlines their goals, timeline, and priorities. Starting with pilot projects in specific areas (e.g., inventory tracking, order picking) can help businesses assess the impact of technology before a full-scale rollout.

Focus on ROI: While the initial investment may seem high, the long-term benefits of smart warehousing technologies far outweigh the costs. By improving efficiency, reducing labor costs, and increasing throughput, companies can achieve a quick return on investment. Business leaders should focus on the ROI potential of smart technology to build support for the transformation.

Engage Employees: The workforce plays a crucial role in the successful adoption of smart technology. Engaging employees in the transition process, providing them with training, and demonstrating the positive impacts of automation on their work lives can increase buy-in and reduce resistance to change.

Leverage Cloud and AI Solutions: Many smart technologies, such as AI-powered WMS, predictive analytics, and cloud-based data platforms, can be implemented without the need for massive infrastructure changes. Cloud-based solutions also offer scalability and flexibility, making them an excellent starting point for businesses looking to embrace digital transformation without committing to major capital expenditures.

Stay Ahead of Emerging Trends: The pace of technological innovation in logistics and supply chain management is accelerating. To stay competitive, businesses should keep an eye on emerging trends like 5G, edge computing, and blockchain, which are expected to further revolutionize warehouse operations. Proactively adopting these technologies will position businesses as leaders in the industry.

Final Thoughts

Smart warehousing is no longer a luxury or a passing trend—it's becoming a necessity for companies that want to remain competitive in the global supply chain. The benefits of smart technologies in warehousing are clear: increased efficiency, cost savings, improved accuracy, and enhanced customer satisfaction. These advantages provide businesses with a significant competitive edge, helping them to streamline operations, respond quickly to changes in demand, and enhance collaboration across the supply chain.

As businesses look toward the future, the adoption of smart technologies in warehouse management will be essential to maintaining a competitive edge. Companies that invest in automation, AI, IoT, and other advanced technologies will be better positioned to navigate the complexities of modern supply chains, meet customer expectations, and achieve sustainable growth. The future of warehousing is digital, and embracing smart technology today will prepare businesses for the challenges and opportunities of tomorrow.

Additional Sections:

❖ *Glossary of Smart Warehousing Terms: Define key terms for readers new to the topic.*

❖ *Resources: List of software, automation providers, and platforms for further learning.*

❖ *Appendix: Templates, checklists, and assessment tools for smart warehouse readiness.*

Glossary of Smart Warehousing Terms

A glossary provides a helpful guide for readers new to the topic of smart warehousing. Here's a list of key terms and definitions commonly used in the industry:

Automation: The use of technology to perform tasks with minimal human intervention. In warehousing, this often involves robotic arms, conveyors, and automated guided vehicles (AGVs).

Automated Guided Vehicles (AGVs): Mobile robots that navigate warehouse floors to transport goods without human intervention. They can follow predetermined paths or use sensors to avoid obstacles.

Artificial Intelligence (AI): A branch of computer science that enables machines to simulate human intelligence. In warehouses, AI helps with demand forecasting, inventory management, and workflow optimization.

Big Data: Large sets of data that can be analyzed to uncover patterns, trends, and associations, especially relating to human behavior and interactions. Big data is critical in optimizing smart warehouse operations.

Internet of Things (IoT): A network of devices connected to the internet, which can collect and exchange data. In smart warehouses, IoT devices can track inventory, monitor equipment, and gather real-time operational data.

Warehouse Management System (WMS): Software that helps manage the day-to-day operations of a warehouse. It tracks inventory, orders, and shipments, and integrates with other smart technologies to optimize warehouse operations.

Digital Twin: A virtual replica of a physical system, used to simulate and test changes in a warehouse environment before implementation. It helps in planning and improving warehouse layouts and operations.

Robotic Process Automation (RPA): The use of robots or software to automate repetitive, rule-based tasks. In warehousing, this can include tasks like sorting and packaging.

Machine Learning (ML): A type of AI where computers learn from large sets of data to improve performance over time without being explicitly programmed. Machine learning can be used in warehouses to predict demand or optimize routing for AGVs.

RFID (Radio Frequency Identification): A technology that uses electromagnetic fields to automatically identify and track tags attached to objects. In warehouses, RFID tags can track inventory and assets.

Cloud Computing: The delivery of computing services such as servers, storage, and databases over the internet. Cloud computing enables smart warehouses to access data remotely and scale operations without significant infrastructure investment.

Lean Warehousing: A methodology aimed at reducing waste in warehouse processes, improving productivity, and maximizing value through continuous improvement practices.

Resources

Below is a list of software, automation providers, and platforms that are essential for businesses interested in adopting smart warehouse solutions:

Warehouse Management Software (WMS) Providers:

SAP EWM: SAP Extended Warehouse Management (EWM) is a powerful WMS that integrates well with other ERP systems and helps streamline warehouse operations.

Oracle WMS: A scalable and flexible warehouse management system that provides real-time inventory tracking and improves operational efficiency.

Manhattan Associates: A leader in warehouse management software, offering solutions that optimize inventory control, order fulfillment, and labor management.

Automation Providers:

Swisslog: Specializes in automated solutions for warehouses, including robotic picking systems and automated storage and retrieval systems (AS/RS).

Kiva Systems (Amazon Robotics): Known for its robotic solutions in warehouse operations, including automated picking and mobile robots that assist with order fulfillment.

Geek+ Robotics: A provider of smart robotics, including Automated Guided Vehicles (AGVs) and sorting robots, designed to optimize warehouse operations.

IoT Platforms and Integration Tools:

ThingWorx: A leading IoT platform that enables warehouse operators to connect, manage, and analyze IoT devices, improving operational insights.

PTC Vuforia: Augmented Reality (AR) tools for training and maintenance, offering solutions that combine IoT and smart technologies for real-time warehouse visibility.

IoT Solutions by Cisco: Cisco provides robust IoT solutions that integrate seamlessly with warehouse management systems, enhancing connectivity and real-time data processing.

AI and Machine Learning Tools:

IBM Watson: A suite of AI-powered tools that can be used to improve demand forecasting, optimize inventory management, and automate decision-making in warehouse environments.

Google Cloud AI: Provides machine learning and predictive analytics tools that can enhance warehouse operations, from predictive maintenance to inventory optimization.

DataRobot: An enterprise AI platform for automating machine learning workflows and providing predictive analytics to optimize supply chain processes, including warehouse management.

Training and Learning Resources:

Coursera: Supply Chain Management Courses: Offers a range of courses related to warehouse management, automation, and smart technologies.

edX: IoT and AI for Logistics: Courses designed to teach professionals how to leverage IoT and AI technologies in warehousing and logistics.

APICS Certification: Provides supply chain management certifications, including those focused on warehouse management systems and technologies.

Appendix

The appendix provides useful templates, checklists, and assessment tools that can guide businesses in assessing their readiness for implementing smart warehouse technologies.

Smart Warehouse Readiness Checklist:

Are current warehouse operations automated or manual?

Do you have the infrastructure to support IoT devices (e.g., sensors, RFID)?

Have you assessed the ROI for implementing smart technologies?

Do you have a clear understanding of AI and machine learning capabilities for inventory management?

Have you identified potential training needs for warehouse staff?

Smart Warehouse Implementation Plan Template:

Phase 1: Initial Assessment and Planning

Evaluate current warehouse systems

Identify pain points and areas for automation

Research potential smart technologies (WMS, IoT, robotics)

Phase 2: Vendor Selection

Evaluate software and hardware providers

Conduct product demos and trials

Select an integration partner

Phase 3: Implementation

Install necessary hardware (robots, sensors, etc.)

Integrate smart systems with existing WMS

Conduct training for staff on new technologies

Phase 4: Testing and Optimization

Run tests to ensure system integration

Optimize processes based on real-time data

Phase 5: Ongoing Maintenance and Continuous Improvement

Monitor system performance

Regularly review and upgrade systems as necessary

Budgeting Template for Smart Warehouse Implementation:

Initial Costs:

Cost of technology and hardware (robots, sensors, WMS)

Infrastructure upgrades (power, network, storage)

Staff training and consultancy fees

Ongoing Costs:

Maintenance and support contracts

Software subscription fees (WMS, IoT platforms)

Energy costs for operating smart systems

Expected Benefits:

ROI from reduced labor costs

Improved inventory accuracy and reduced stockouts

Increased order fulfillment speed

www.ingramcontent.com/pod-product-compliance
Lightning Source LLC
Chambersburg PA
CBHW050006230526
45465CB00003BB/1279